INSPIRATIONS *from* FRANCE & ITALY

INSPIRATIONS *from* FRANCE & ITALY

Betty Lou Phillips

Photography by Dan Piassick

Gibbs Smith, Publisher
TO ENRICH AND INSPIRE HUMANKIND
Salt Lake City   Charleston   Santa Fe   Santa Barbara

First Edition

11 10 09 08 07   5 4 3 2 1

Text © 2007 Betty Lou Phillips
Photographic credits on page 203

Published by

Gibbs Smith, Publisher

P.O. Box 667

Layton, Utah 84041

Orders: 1.800.835.4993

www.gibbs-smith.com

Designed by Cherie Hanson
Printed and bound in China

Library of Congress Cataloging-in-Publication Data

Phillips, Betty Lou.
  Inspirations from France and Italy / Betty Lou
Phillips ; photographs by Danny Piassick. — 1st ed.
    p. cm.
  ISBN-13: 978-1-4236-0205-7
  ISBN-10: 1-4236-0205-6
  1. Interior decoration—United States. 2. Decoration and ornament—France—Influence. 3. Decoration and ornament—Italy—Influence. I. Piassick, Dan. II. Title.

NK2002.P52 2007
747—dc22

                                        2007018394

ON THE FRONT JACKET: *As if defining good taste, bolts of icy, candlelight hues from the fabric house of Christopher Hyland swathe an ottoman and a pair of bergère chairs from the Cameron Collection, Dallas. During the reign of Louis XV (1715–74), the French armchair with exposed wood frame, soft flowing lines and closed upholstered sides made a grand entrance. The sterling silver tea service is from the Italian firm Buccellati, revered for superb artisanship.*

ON THE BACK JACKET: *One could feast on the architecture alone. Island Architects in La Jolla designed the California villa. In the same town is Chandelier, the maker of the iron fixture. Brunschwig & Fils covers chairs.*

END PAPERS: *Acclaimed Fortuny fabrics are an Italian hallmark. "Campanelle" is a seventeenth-century design with a morning glory motif.*

TITLE PAGE: *Practicing what author Edith Wharton preached in The Decoration of Houses, timeless French style resides inside—appropriate to the architecture of the house. Nevertheless, modern-day comfort starts at the front door, satisfying needs.*

OPPOSITE: *A regal breakfast room overlooks a stunning swimming pool and manicured grounds. Chairs by Patina surround the Erika Brunson table. Couch, Ltd., hand stitched the curtains, using Rose Tarlow Textiles and West Coast Trimmings.*

Contents

Catering to the homeowners' wishes, a functional and aesthetically pleasing kitchen integrates the surrounding butler's pantry, breakfast room and sitting area, while wood floors add warmth. Pendant lights are from Peck & Co.; hand-painted tiles are from Architectural Design Resources, both in Houston. On windows: Osborne & Little fabric and Travers trim.

Acknowledgments

ONE OF THE NICEST ASPECTS of writing a book is the opportunity to meet and get to know so many interesting people. Special thanks, therefore, goes to those from New York to California who opened the doors to their splendid *chateaux, palazzi,* villas and vacation homes and permitted us to photograph their residences: Maria and Michael Ainbinder, Anita and Thurman Arnold, Candi and Dr. Rick Blau, Jo Beth and Berry Cash, Pam and Tim Culver, Ruth Ann and Mark Dunn, Kim and Scott Martin, Connie and Bill McNally, Connie and Brooks Noah, Ellen and John Rutherford, Bridget and Jim Tanner, Meredith and Bill Tichenor and more.

I appreciate, too, the effort the following designers put into creating the alluring, satisfying rooms that make up this book: Shannon Bowers, Dan Brady, Cathryn Chapman, Laura Lee Clark, Holly Lydick,

Sophisticated silk velvet curtains, edged in a Scalamandré trim, and a vintage récamier from Shabby Slip, New Orleans, capture the romance of Italy. A portrait of Madame Récamier by French artist Jacques-Louis David hangs in the Louvre. Emperor Napoléon Bonaparte (1769–1821) exiled the provocative Parisian madame in 1805; however, after his defeat at Waterloo in 1815, she returned to the city and resumed her salon.

Stephanie Moore, Connie McNalley, Linda McCormick, Constance Noah, Christina Phillips, Marilyn Phillips and Mary Lee Singer.

Also, I am personally grateful to those who facilitated the timely completion of homes so my own projects could become an integral part of this book. Actually, we might still be shooting were it not for Donna Burley, Laura Elms, Mark Farmer, Esther Gandal, Jesus Marroquin, Philip Minton, Jodie Newby and Linda Swain, who often accomplished the incredible, rallying to this cause. Special thanks also go to Jennifer Chapman, Frieda Heath, Angela Malone, Ron Mutcher and Jayne Taylor.

It truly takes a village to produce a book. For her invaluable research support, I thank Janice Stuerzl—and for their prized design assistance, I thank Tara Kohlbacher, Julie Macatee, Andrea Smith and Missy Williams. Also, I'd like to express my gratitude to photographer Dan Piassick for his patience, open-mindedness and, most importantly, talent, to say nothing of his amazing rapport with animals, which certainly helped make our photo shoots successful.

Add to the above list a love and appreciation for my long-time editor, Madge Baird, and her admirable team. Also, I sincerely thank you, the reader, for so kindly inviting *Inspirations from France & Italy* into your home.

Introduction

ONE PICTURE IS WORTH TEN THOUSAND WORDS, says a Chinese proverb. And it is safe to say that the familiar adage proves true. A room in print worthy of Paris's beguiling Right Bank or of Florence, the heart of the Tuscany region where the presence of artists Leonardo da Vinci and Michelangelo still looms, catches knowing eyes and almost surely inspires creative minds.

But the power of pictures isn't new. Hundreds of years ago, scattered Native American tribes speaking various languages painted pictographs on cave walls, rocks, and hides to communicate their thoughts, needs and feelings. Nowadays images spread across the glossy pages of widely read shelter magazines and coveted design books have equally grand, if different, ambitions. With pitching imitation as the sincerest form of flattery decidedly last-century, most savvy publications reflecting luxury lifestyles appear intent, instead, on urging readers to fashion their own unmistakably swank empires, whether *châteaux*, villas or *palazzi*.

Never mind that in bastions that want for nothing, a coterie of magnetic antiques—exquisite tapestries, dramatic chandeliers and storied armoires set amid sensuously sculpted statuary—are expected fixtures. Or that their signature siblings—swaths of fabrics from prestigious European mills replete with attention-grabbing *passementerie*—are just as likely the focus. All look equally at home on this side of the Atlantic as they do overseas and, more importantly, fulfill an American penchant for timeless grandeur that never wanes.

Lately, though, it seems that old-world artistry is not enough for a sizable and growing number of design aficionados. For many of us, satisfaction comes from creating cosmopolitan glamour—a chic blend of the traditional and edgy with a downtown attitude apt for an era with more choices than ever.

Keeping pace with Paris, labor-intensive Venetian plaster walls plus sofas and fabrics by J. Robert Scott and Larsen simply complement each other rather than court attention. Also in vogue: French furniture that harks back to the 1940s, finished in silver leaf. Mirrored tables with antique glass are from the Paris Moderne Collection by John Himmel, available to the trade at David Sutherland, Dallas. Threatening to steal the spotlight, however, is the antique limestone cheminée. Dallas's RF Imports unearthed the fireplace in the Normandy region of France.

After dismissing polarized notions about what understated elegance means or doesn't mean, we welcome the best France and Italy have to offer, give considerable thought to striking reminders from other far-flung cultures and take the Greek dramatist Aristophanes' challenge to heart: "Let each man exercise the art he knows," he famously said. And we do. Layering panache and pizzazz with varying degrees of theatrical dash, we trust our instincts to pair what we were unable to resist in our travels amidst what we already own—and in a break with tradition ease the formality of sophisticated European décor.

Predictably, then, it is only fitting when crafting a design book to honor this achievement. To manage that, my assistants and I scout homes until we have a database of dozens of memorable interiors unlikely to be labeled stuffy, much less ordinary. Broadly chronicling our preferences, we appreciate the comfort that no camera can quite capture, focus on how a room functions as well as how it appears, and favor unexpected details that in general raise any environment above the fray. That we are far from blasé about billowing window treatments that look as if fabricated by one of France's *petits mains,* the highly-skilled seamstresses who hand-stitch haute couture ball gowns, is obvious—as is a bias for our own work.

More often than not, we shun interiors that overflow with objects, which we cannot help thinking fail to foster a serene feeling of well-being. Our mind-set is definitely "less is more." How else to explain why we shy away from shooting any setting that looks as if it is mounting an exhibition to a celebrated monarch's influence? This doesn't mean we are put off by antiques any more than agree with the contention espoused by the French that one should not tamper with furniture whether or not time has taken a toll. Regardless, we are the first to admit that interesting back stories, such as surviving the French Revolution and two World Wars, add to their allure.

Actually, photographing a home is not as easy as it looks. To the owner's credit, windows gleam (unless it has recently rained), silver shines, crystal sparkles and beds tout freshly ironed fine linens by the time we arrive. In addition, the family dog typically appears recently groomed. But even if not, he or she still is sure to melt our hearts as we set out readying the site for its photo "op," aiming to keep the gaggle of telephones, televisions, and computers that come in all persuasions away from the telling lenses of our cameras, thinking nothing of physically removing them when we can. And when we can't do that we use Photoshop, a program that allows us to take out recessed ceiling lights, wall switches, registers and temperature controls, which can be distracting. Somewhere along the way, we learned that a melted ice cube will help do away with an indention left by a furniture leg and restore the carpet pile.

Although rearranging has its limits, necessity requires that for visual impact we fill empty spaces that loom large and remove objects that the viewfinder has difficulty interpreting—or, more accurately, "reading." Before the photographer snaps a picture, we also spin lamp shades until seams are hidden, tape lamp cords so they don't dangle and try hiding wall outlets. Despite the weather, a warm fire may glow in the hearth rather than risk having readers look into a black hole.

Given the influence that pictures hold, it is only natural that no one would dare sit on either the sofas or chairs until long after the camera stops clicking. And that we would find other ways to help furniture and accessories gain the camera's approval, such as rousing pillow flanges from hibernation with tape, plumping and propping throws and lighting rooms just so.

Is it any wonder, then, that one picture can wordlessly offer a stream of bright ideas? Or that we bowed to this prevailing wisdom and shepherded into print rooms that present ultimate proof of the ancient adage? Setting one well-appointed space apart from others is a distinctive way of defining style, which invariably communicates the thoughts, needs and feelings of those raising families, welcoming friends and celebrating meaningful occasions in these environments. That these interiors owe more than a little to influences from France and Italy, and sometimes England, Portugal and Spain, is noticeable. But a still closer look at the photographs reveals that aesthetic inspiration can spring from anywhere—cultures as diverse as India, China, Egypt and Turkey—with or without traveling to these places. Clearly, we've moved well beyond honoring one French monarch and including the expected Italian painted piece; though, of course, we still cherish evidence of both.

I hope the images that follow will stretch your imagination, suggest fresh ways of artfully enhancing your surroundings, and, of course, ultimately satisfy your soul. For, according to the nineteenth-century French writer Marie-Henri Beyle (1783–1842), better known by his pen name Stendhal, "Beauty is the promise of happiness." Certainly, there is no reason not to take him at his word. After all, one picture is still worth ten thousand words.

—*Betty Lou Phillips, ASID*

A confidante—with numerous seats attached in a single unit—exudes an aristocratic air as Fortuny underscores its glamour. The workshops of world-renowned Fortuny are on the Venetian island of Giudecca.

13

French Flair

Much has changed since Louis XIV (1643–1715), Louis XV (1715–74) and Louis XVI (1774–92) unabashedly drenched the Palace of Versailles in gilded excess, provoking a revolution that brought the monarchy tumbling down and prompted habitués of all economic levels—poor, middle class and rich—aspiring for better lives to famously proclaim *"liberté, égalité, et fraternité!"* the national mantra.

Today mega-mansions, however worthy of American fantasies, fail to denote either wealth or privilege in the Ile-de-France—the historic heart of the country encompassing Paris and surrounding seven *départements* (districts). The populous hub of much of France's cultural, educational, financial and political power has its own set of symbols that are not only the ultimate measure of status but also much more discreet than those in the States.

Heaven forbid that any of the eleven million men and women in this region, or at least many of them, would be so déclassé as

À la française, a petit salon is the epitome of old-world grace replete with fabrics from Christopher Hyland, sofas from the Cameron Collection, throws by Fortuny and, notably, an elongated pillow hand-painted by Carlsbad, California, artist Jennifer Chapman. Rich paint finishes are by Jo Mattison, Dallas. The walnut commode is eighteenth-century French. Gilded mirrors from the same period are Italian. Thanks to Carol Piper Rugs, Houston, a circa 1890 carpet from Agra—home of India's admirable Taj Mahal—lends a surplus of grandeur.

15

to chase American dreams—private jets or "fractional" shares of them, jaw-dropping yachts, flashy cars or sprawling vacation homes—any more than spend a fortune extensively renovating or restoring a primary property down its cracked marble floors before ambitiously decorating it. (In the interest of equality, the Fifth Republic ideal ignores religious and ethnic differences, so those with residency papers exude a collective identity regardless of their origin. Officially, all citizens are French whether they share or distance themselves from Gallic values.)

With ongoing sympathies to the principles that led to the French Revolution, like-minded style setters determinedly try to distance themselves from the *ancien regimes*' vaunted reputation for over-the-top displays of rococo extravagance that roused feelings of resentment outside Versailles' walls and resulted in a torturous uprising.

Not that the socially ambitious don't find acceptable ways to separate themselves from their neighbors. Or that there aren't touches of glamour inside *appartements* in the Ile-de-France, where by some estimates nearly 75 percent of the inhabitants dwell. Although the practice of creating period rooms that drip in brocades and gold leaf is virtually extinct, instantly identifiable symbols of style and sophistication—such as eighteenth-century furniture, paintings and porcelain, luxurious textiles and *passementerie*—inspired by the royals are coveted and collected. Much like the fine linens and heirloom silver passed down from father to son, mother to daughter, all are celebrated badges of the privileged class with bearing on how one is perceived. > 22

Giving a salon with old-world élan new perspective are chairs in the style of LVI from Nancy Corzine, Los Angeles, dressed by Bangkok-based silk manufacturer Jim Thompson. The window treatment highlights the trend in both France and Italy away from over-the-top curtains, meaning swags, valances, and jabots. And while on the topic of trends, the Labrador retriever is the purebred of the moment, according to the American Kennel Club. (The Yorkshire terrier is next most popular.)

An eighteenth-century armoire from Jacqueline Adams Antiques in Atlanta pays homage to France with its magnificence. Palatially proportioned armoires with deep, intricate carving, piercing, shaped bonnets (curved tops) and the patina of time are the most celebrated sources of Gallic pride. But with le tout Paris in a perpetual quest for the best, to say nothing of American interest in fine French furniture, similar pieces are not easily surrendered, never mind easy to find.

A Paris flea market find known in France as a surtout, meaning "above all," according to the dealer, hosts vases from Takashamaya, New York City. An imperial mirror adds further drama.

Strands of myriad influences add more than a bit of distinction. Dallas decorative artist Jo Mattison used Schaibin leaf, a Japanese technique, to produce the metallic-finished gold leaf walls. Iron rods are by Palmer Design, San Diego. The aged, finely woven rug came from the Lahore region of India, now Pakistan, via Carol Piper, whose Houston shop wears her name.

In matters material, however, nothing manages to vault status-conscious habitués to the top of the social pyramid quite like dwelling in a handsome Haussmann-era *appartement* with enviable fourteen-foot ceilings, deep chiseled moldings, patterned wood floors and imposing fireplaces, obviously sans the commercial kitchens, home theaters and his and her offices that are commonplace in luxury American residences.

During the Second Empire (1852–70), Louis-Napoléon Bonaparte III, the nephew of Napoléon I, hired Baron Haussmann to revamp the ravaged, war-torn capital with squalid housing into the most elegant, imperial city on earth. But for all Baron Haussmann's efforts—banishing thousands of unsightly structures and rebuilding the city in a cohesive style with limestone masonry rising no more than six stories tall—evidence suggests that savvy city dwellers of all socioeconomic classes are less interested in elevating their status by perching in the epitome of old-world elegance within one of the French capital's affluent *arrondissements* (divisions of *départements*) than intent on being recognized and admired for their personal flair.

To state the obvious, neither social cachet nor wealth is a prerequisite of commendable taste. Naturally, money does create the freedom to purchase what one wants. But when it comes to making a positive impression, neither a royal budget nor living just steps from the Seine necessarily buys *bon goût*—long the center of the much-lauded Gallic approach to dressing, dining and entertaining, which are as distinctive as their decorating. > 39

OPPOSITE: *No matter that the well-coiffed hairstyles of King Louis XVI of France and oft-maligned Queen Marie Antoinette have fallen from favor. An eighteenth-century walnut commode ensures this powder room maintains a majestic air. Regal amenities—a gilded sink, rock crystal fittings, sconces and a chandelier, all from Sherle Wagner—further the illusion of glamour any royal or commoner would envy.*

BELOW: *Custom gold embroidery elevates linen hand towels to a fashion statement. Invité, in essence, means "invited guest."*

The shift away from dated skirted tables has prompted strong demand for antique bar carts, which are both functional and fashionable. One crafted in heavy-gauge brass steals this media room's show. It is from K&M Antiques of London in Manhattan. Fabric from Mokum Textiles covers chairs. Brass pole lamp is by Vaughan.

OPPOSITE: A cleverly concealed flat-screen television turns a family room into a screening room that dazzles audiences. Both walls and sofas flaunt Nobilis fabrics—perfectly aligned at seams. The amethyst (quartz) rock crystal votives are by Jon McCoy.

French style and time-worn charm meet in a sitting room off the kitchen where pots de confit—once used for preserving duck or goose for the South of France specialty cassoulet—share shelf space with neatly arranged books.

OPPOSITE: *Confit jars create a vignette atop an eighteenth-century bonnetière—a tall, narrow cabinet sufficiently deep to hold woven goods, bonnets or a television—all culled from French Country Interiors, Dallas.*

Reportedly, we spend one-third of our lives in bed; so it is only natural that our affection for upscale amenities is strong. Both the sensuous bed and bombé—meaning bulging or rounded—chest were hand painted in Venice for Patina, Atlanta. Also works of art are pale gold fabrics from Christopher Hyland and linens by D. Porthault—woven, finished and embroidered in the company's factories outside Paris.

Since the fourteenth century, Europeans have coveted noble, hand-woven tapestries. And these days, Americans often have them at the top of acquisitions lists. Weavers once wandered from place to place, settling temporarily in the château, church or monastery where they received a commission after presenting detailed paintings or drawings called "cartoons," from which they would then copy chosen patterns. A leopard runner from Patterson, Flynn & Martin ascends the staircase with effortless ease.

RIGHT: No less regal than the headboard is the Patina footboard.

FAR RIGHT: Touting Nobilis fabric, an inviting Summer Hill chaise offers an ideal place for reading books, listening to music or talking on the telephone. Adding dash: a cashmere throw by D. Porthault. Inspired by the Impressionists, the French firm was the first to introduce printed bed linens.

For all the apparent affluence at the Palace of Versailles, Louis XVI was the first French king to have a complete cabinet de bains, or bathroom, with running water. Both he and his controversial queen each had a sterling silver bathtub (melted after the monarchy fell to help repay debts accrued during the French Revolution). Flanking the antique mirror shown here are fancy amenities and Murano sconces, reflecting traditional Venetian techniques passed down over centuries.

OPPOSITE: A former hall radiates glamour after jettisoning its sole closet and morphing into a dressing room, with a hand-blown Murano glass chandelier. Burnished gold gimp embellishes walls upholstered over batting in a silk by Kravet. Mirrored doors wear Swarovski crystal knobs, a cut above the rest. Iconic brown and beige tote and Pegasus luggage are from Louis Vuitton, the French luxury goods purveyor established in 1854 that still sells the same trunks and handbags that Empress Eugénie favored during the Second Empire.

A milk chocolate stripe from Perennials, Dallas, and striking stainless steel desk from les années quarante—or the French 1940s —masterfully crafted by Michael Shannon & Associates, San Francisco, gives a small office a fashionable, artsy edge. Decorator's Walk sofa fabric is from Belgium; Ankasa pillows were hand-stitched in India. The bar cart is old, but the new favorite adornment. Natura carpet is from Stark.

BELOW: With a bit of attitude, tiebacks from the Paris flea market dazzle beyond the ordinary.

33

A door leads to a bathroom for campers. And with all due respect to the traditional shower curtain, a fun alternative—hand painted by Dallas artist Gillian Bradshaw Smith—makes a bigger splash.

After a fun-filled day, some campers can sleep soundly most anywhere. However, high and mighty La Lune bunk beds suggest lodgings a little homier. The Steiff bear ambled in from FAO Schwarz, N.Y. Dallas-based artist Kay Fox treated the walls. A stump from a fallen tree now serves as the end table. Grommets add dimension to the pure cotton that Henry Calvin Fabrics supplied for the shade.

In a bathroom that works with the bedroom, lighting fixtures are from Murray's Iron Works, Los Angeles.

OPPOSITE: It is a jungle out there, but this spot is a true refuge—animal refuge, that is, where sightings are far from rare. Leslie Hannon brush fringe takes Travers' tiger chenille in a playful direction. Meanwhile, an unseen elephant proves tame. Madagascar, the remote island in the Indian Ocean off South Africa, inspired the Summer Hill natural grass cloth climbing the walls. Budgie handcrafted the four-poster bed from ecologically friendly bamboo stalks in the Philippine Islands.

As if Old MacDonald is trying to spiff up his farm, Hinson loden-green corduroy—fittingly durable—bunks on a Charles P. Rogers bed propped against glazed pine-paneled walls. The suede bedskirt is by Kravet, paisley curtain fabric by Christopher Hyland and natural sisal from Stark Carpet. Charm resides in an antique stove, plus the irresistible barnyard animals adopted from FAO Schwarz, New York.

For the most part, however, each region has a well-defined identity grounded in tradition that developed centuries ago, when the terrain made trade between villages impractical and limited the exchange of ideas. Even if modern technology has increasingly exposed habitués to the broader world, the majority of French are reluctant to give up part of their heritage. Until the mid-twentieth century, regional dialects endured, and still, area dwellings often have a similar recognizable exterior look. Time-honored *vaisseliers* (hutches), armoires and *chiffonières* (chests of drawers) made from indigenous materials resolutely bring local flavor to environments. To be sure, one does not decorate the same way in Alsace as, say, in the area of Provence known as the Lubéron, or in the Côte d'Azure as in Brittany; though, certainly, within an area, design practices reflect an array of lifestyles.

Perhaps it follows, then, that those who live in the Ile-de-France—or at least some of them—at times take to the streets to pressure the government into backing down from unpopular policies, mostly subscribe to restrained elegance and yet, just as strikingly, opt to build on the ideals of the long-dead Bourbon monarchs. In other words, as if decreed from on high, the French remain true to the following design principles:

Quality is paramount. Back in the eighteenth century, France astounded the world with her exquisite artisanship, setting standards of excellence previously unseen in Italy and Spain while bringing the style of her people global acclaim. And it is fair to say that nothing has changed. Savoring the same remarkable artistry that became a hallmark of prestige, > 45

First impressions count, so an entry is an ideal place to make a grand statement. Dissimilar eighteenth-century Louis XV walnut commodes, both from Orion Antiques, Dallas, are at home in New York. Shades by Bella Copia, San Francisco, bedeck stone lamps from Panache, Los Angeles. A chenille damask from the English manufacturer James Brindley of Harrogate, wraps a settee from Jacqueline Adams Antiques, Atlanta. Wall covering from Gracie, founded in 1898, lines the walls.

OPPOSITE: An antique bibliothèque of French Country Interiors descent holds a collection of faïence, the French name for Faenza, an Italian pottery center that produced painted majolica ware—on opaque, pure white ground earthenware—for export as early as the fifteenth century. Pitchers, soup tureens and platters are from Neal & Co., Houston. The walnut Portuguese table and French chairs are by Hamilton, Inc., Los Angeles. The latter bask in Jim Thompson and Coraggio Textiles. Chandelier and altar sticks are from Jacqueline Adams Antiques, Atlanta.

A nineteenth-century tapestry discovered at the Paris flea market is worthy of pride of place in a New York dining room. Until King Henri IV (1533–1610) lured Brussels' most highly skilled weavers to Paris, Belgium dominated the European tapestry market. Then in 1662, influenced by his grandfather, Louis XIV (1638–1715) assured the supremacy of French tapestries by fusing the finest weavers under one roof at Les Gobelins—the former residence of the Gobelins family—and by appointing as director the celebrated royal painter Charles Le Brun (1619–90).

OPPOSITE: *Another view of the dining room on page 40.*

42

With unabashed glamour and everyday practicality, an easily maintained mirrored coffee table is a welcome addition to a sunroom where the family gathers. Sofa is upholstered in fabric by Manuel Canovas; chairs wear Vervain. Zimmer + Rohde shades control the light.

each new generation that comes of age struggles to embrace the best furnishings it can manage as if with every choice assuming responsibility for the country's ongoing dignity—which is, of course, the intention.

The past must be present. Whether longing for a major piece of furniture or an *objet d'art*, reverence for the past exerts a pull so strong that for many it is unthinkable to live among meaningless pieces having no ties to their heritage or, worse, in a house pulled together at a hurried pace with furnishings lacking familiar signs of wear. Filling empty rooms with shiny new reproductions is at odds with a culture notoriously hard to please, not to mention famously hostile to copies lacking the workmanship that only master artisans can deliver and it is schooled to recognize. Indeed, Gauls are quick to admit that age alone is no guarantee of quality any more than is old-world joinery, though most feel the old is likely to increase in value while the new does not necessarily lead to added worth.

Settings should evolve over time. It is entirely apt, then, that rooms are often works in varying stages of progress, hinting of possibilities. While some people simply bide their time, pinning hopes on wishes to be fulfilled, countless others choose to allow one idea to inspire another, letting their visions slowly take shape. (Still others, of course, simply prefer living in well-edited, streamlined spaces that keep furnishings in check.) Whatever the case, the way the majority see it, the most admirable quarters look as if they have been furnished piece by piece over several lifetimes rather than pulled together overnight. > 50

A need for storage space led to an eighteenth-century bonnetière joining this chic home. The résumé of the chandelier reads like that of an international diplomat, as it traveled from the French-Belgian border to the Paris flea market prior to winging its way to Atlanta, then stopping in Dallas—before finally settling in a community just outside of New York City.

Emily, the irresistible monkey with a taste for beignets, tutus and mischief, springs from the pages of "Emily Goes Wild" by Betty Lou Phillips into a Summer Hill chaise. Her next stop? Paris, no less, toting along her power to amuse and characteristic grand style, though a map of the City of Light is the ideal travel partner. Not until the nineteenth century were maps printed in color.

OPPOSITE: *Dolled up in pink and chocolate brown, this young girl's room is both smart and irresistibly sweet. Bolts of billowing sheer from the French house of Etamine—with taffeta underpinnings—bring a fanciful touch to the custom bed from Michael Shannon & Associates, San Francisco. Bedskirt check is by Brunschwig & Fils, founded in France more than a century ago. Paint is Benjamin Moore—HC 76, Davenport Tan.*

Sporting a solid brass plaque that reads "Paris 1930," a metal cabinet stepped out of a post office in the City of Light seemingly prepared to hold most everything a teenager might own. The find is from Skelton St. John, Houston.

OPPOSITE: An old iron stove sides a Charles P. Rogers bed, outfitted in a Beacon Hill plaid, Kravet solid and linens from Yves Delorme. Poised nearby are the latest in a string of trophies won playing chess. FYI: The most humongous chessboard stands in the main square in the medieval town of Maròstica, Italy. On the second weekend in September, only in even-numbered years, costumed people reenact a local legend by standing in as chess pieces.

More than necessity must prompt the desire to buy. In a nation where perception is an issue taken seriously, self-restraint seemingly is an ingrained Gallic trait—a deterrent embedded in the national psyche. People are capable of living for years without a carpet, tapestry, commode or other furnishing until one comes along with the requisite French origin and a certain *je ne sais quois* that makes the piece clearly worth the wait. Purchasing frivolously or buying second best is not in the Gaullist tradition. In fact, the latter begets short-lived joy, equating to a pricey lesson in the view of many.

Heirlooms merit a prominent spot. As a rule, settings start with furnishings passed down from one generation to the next, often with stories, whether true or not. As rooms take shape, they gather even more accoutrements rooted in the past. While Americans may border on being emotionally detached, tossing aside offerings that are not exactly what is fancied—if accepted at all—the French hunger for tangible links to beloved ancestors who lived centuries apart. (With tradition weighing heavily, most are especially discreet if circumstances necessitate parting with a family heirloom, in hopes of not raising eyebrows.)

Not only that, but there is broad agreement that hand-me-downs from family must occupy a privileged place, even if they fail to measure up to notions of Parisian elegance. No matter that these legacies might appear to need some cosmetic help. The reassuring feeling of the familiar is comforting. Besides, in French minds, signs of time rather than painstaking restorations bent on stripping away years add to a furnishing's old-world panache. Regardless that a piece may be somewhat

A staircase leading from the first floor to the second offers a spot to admire the view. Fabrics are by Old World Weavers.

OPPOSITE: *An artfully fashioned entry brims with culture and charm, as France, Portugal and America each have their say.*

KOSTABI

Light pours into a living room/ study where style flows from a penchant for detail. Robert Allen Fabrics cover chairs. Milk chocolate walls with a blue glaze serve as a backdrop for gatherings, thanks to Segretto Finishes, Houston.

overwhelming for its less-roomy new setting. Thrust into a prominent spot, it garners certain deference by virtue of its age.

Size matters. For centuries now, a propensity for heroic-sized pieces that lend distinction has held sway. Since many dwellings remain in the same family for generations, some furnishings never need be moved from one address to another. But the old-world élan of other interiors may well owe more to the fact that the need for imposing pieces remains etched in minds, largely unchanged despite the sale of *châteaux* with punishing overhead gradually yielding to less-spacious homes with smaller rooms more readily maintained.

Clearly, few furnishings suitable for a sumptuous château are equally appropriate for an *appartement*; yet, given that French eyes are accustomed to seeing furniture with presence, somehow they manage to enlarge the perception of an area. It is almost as if rallying nobly to prevent, say, a rock crystal chandelier, *bibliothèque* (literally, library), *buffet deux corps* (literally, buffet two bodies) or other iconic national symbol from being snapped up by a wave of foreign tourists clamoring for French antiques. This, indeed, is a concern for a people who see themselves as guardians of their heritage.

Balance is key to creating a feeling of well-being. Unless furnishings with towering demeanors find their way to the right places, their considerable presence can be off-putting, jarringly slanting the visual weight to one side of a room. It is not by accident, then, that ancestral portraits—for which there seems to be no shortage of fondness—pose arrogantly on easels, taut

Nail heads draw attention to the shape of a custom piano bench.

OPPOSITE: *The view from the entry leads to the music room and into the dining room, lending ceremony to an architecturally linked space that revels in antique French armchairs decked in a Hinson crewel. While Americans often favor open floor plans, Europeans prefer that stately doors define areas. Chandeliers are from Paul Ferrante, Los Angeles.*

tapestries look down from walls and folding screens brushed with painted scenes clamor visibly for the spotlight across the room from statuary. Or that oils, gouaches, and prints swell into collections, stretching toward the sky. Though none may tote equalizing weight, each helps view exalted, attention-commanding neighbors in a more flattering light. Not that there need be something in every corner, basking in a majestic mirror's reflected glow—or that striking a proper balance is easy even for the French.

Harmony is more important than conformity. Many, if not most, would no more purchase a bedroom "suite" than a so-called dining room "set" with wood finishes boringly alike. As for lamps, the majority of them tend to be unique. And while Americans may flaunt five-piece place settings of the same china, the French take a dim view of matching tableware, preferring instead, compatible pattern mixes. In those residences that want for nothing, disparate elements, each with its own centuries-long résumé, come together in a sophisticated way.

What's more, elegance must mingle with ease. Even when settings exude a glamour few can ignore, convention dictates possessions must represent a culture that prizes understatement, which means weaving the unassuming with that more grand or, if one will, mixing princely furnishings with humble finds every bit as fascinating.

Layering old-world comfort with nineteenth- and twentieth-century furnishings gives a newly constructed French château the underpinnings of age. The earthy palette includes textured fabrics from George Smith, Brunschwig & Fils, Highland Court and Glant. The area rug is seagrass. The hand-forged iron chandelier is antique, from Brown, Houston.

Contrasting finishes and collectibles are the foundation of a kitchen with the conveniences of today but with an appeal that would rival one in France.

OPPOSITE: *In collaboration with nature, Houston architect Ken Newberry gives the breakfast room of a French château authentic character and charm. Walls are Granbury stone, the same material as the façade of the house. The farm table, circa 1850, is from Neal & Co., Houston. Ladder-back chairs flaunt fabric from Rose Tarlow Textiles. (As if on cue, the family dog wandered in for a glimpse of what was going on——and decided to stay.)*

Appropriately then, the precious sit politely near the less pricey, the ordinary across the room from the extraordinary, each attracting interest now and then. Some finer things, such as *trumeaux* (painted overmantels), *bureau-plats* (writing tables) and shapely clocks—seventeenth-century inventions—do demand more than their fair share of attention. It is not fitting, however, for living quarters to brim with precious objects exhibited like museum artifacts jostling for the limelight.

An artfully assembled collection is fundamental. Collectors second to none, the French are constantly on the hunt, swarming to their favorite shopping places, starting with the famed *Marché aux Puces* in the village of Saint-Ouen, just north of Paris, and the flea market in the Provençal town of L'Isle-sur-la-Sorgue, a twenty-minute drive from Avignon. Aspiring for a collected rather than decorated look, they also relentlessly comb diverse open-air markets held on weekends throughout the year.

For the most part, pilgrimages to *vide-greniers* (empty attics, literally) promise disparate finds, from the expected to the intriguing to the surprising. *Foires de brocante*, or fairs selling secondhand goods, also lend a versatile decorating hand with an expansive array of modestly priced treats. And for serious shoppers who fancy top-end collectibles and aren't overly concerned about price, there are *salons d'antiquité*.

Given their strong sense of self, commanding flair and, not least, *savoir-faire*, most are not the sort to turn over accessorizing a home, never mind furnishing it, to a decorator. In their view,

Waiting to be noticed: a collection of antique Italian candlesticks and prickets—early candlesticks with spikes projecting above the rim—sit on a console in the style of Louis XV by Dennis & Leen.

OPPOSITE: *An eighteenth-century tapestry adds old-world panache to a Stateside entry free of drafts, unlike in châteaux, where these early works of art warmed walls. Aged wooden piers hail from Thailand.*

this leaves one vulnerable to uncertain results; so, not surprisingly, most prefer to make a statement on their own.

Finally, unexpected embellishments project a regal air, to say nothing of making an abiding impression. Armed with artistic, educated eyes, unerring taste and amazing confidence, the French predictably look to their heritage for inspiration. In the seventeenth century, Louis XIV and his visionary finance minister, Jean-Baptist Colbert, established a strictly controlled guild system that regulated the work of artisans, raising the specialties at which they excelled to even higher standards. More than three centuries later, the Sun King's perfectionism remains his extraordinary gift to France. Though his penchant for extravagance may be better known, King Louis XIV deserves credit for influencing most everything the French do. From their insistence on finely crafted furniture and regal textiles to turning out rooms with dignity and panache, the French unparalleled attention to detail that borders on obsession is a testimony to the late king's fastidiousness.

Masterfully cut, flawlessly tailored window treatments brush the floor—with braid or fringe trimming drizzled from pencil-thin piped edging, adding a distinctive touch. (Valances and other exaggerated looks are out.) In a stream of perfectly matched seams, fabrics that include story-telling toiles affectionately hug upholstery; though in less-dressy spaces tailor tucks often nestle in shapely slipcovers, as unassuming seagrass offhandedly blankets well-traveled floors. Polished brass grilles with scrolled motifs adorn heating vents, elevating the ordinary, while leopard prints relax the seriousness of rooms with a trace of playfulness.

Now, there is jewelry for the floor. Hand-forged hardware from the sixteenth-century inspired this pewter grate by Brad Oldham, Dallas. The master artisan sculpts, hand casts and hand finishes custom pieces.

OPPOSITE: *Gleaming Venetian plaster plus sophisticated furnishings— console, mirror and bench—from Le Louvre Antiques, Dallas, impart high style with a modern edge. Powder room hardware is by Sherle Wagner.*

Whereas small paintings would disappear in soaring spaces, massed together *salon* style (stacked high on walls and over doors) they make a strong statement. Suggesting the sophistication of a bygone era, several rock-crystal chandeliers may drift overhead in the same room, as sconces wash walls with light.

In a testament to France's artistic past, no detail escapes scrutiny. Surely, nothing is left to chance. Perhaps it's no surprise, then, that many historians say France has long had a love-hate relationship with its aristocratic heritage. Though the Revolution supposedly squashed desire for frivolous excesses and set the nation on a new course, by all appearances, many French citizens are struggling with their identity. While well aware of what it means to be French, they feel a need to apologize for their former monarchs' extravagant trappings and take pains to underplay their wealth. Yet they continue under a spell, adhering to the aesthetic practices championed by Louis XIV, Louis XV and Louis XVI—who ultimately influence both their taste and the manner in which they live.

The walls of a television room come to life, thanks to Dallas artist Jacki Musso. Fabric on chairs is from Larsen. Koplavitch and Zimmer flows from windows. The bronze chandelier is from Donald J. Embree Antiques, Dallas. Arrangement is by Todd Design Creative Services, also in Dallas.

Savonnerie and Aubusson Carpets

They are art underfoot, sophisticated, deftly woven narratives widely heralded as France's most opulent textile. They are, of course, Savonnerie carpets—deep piled and hand knotted—made of fine wools and natural dyes.

In 1604, a headstrong eighteen-year-old named Pierre Dupont (1577–1640) announced his intention to produce handmade carpets rivaling the quality of those from the East, which the French had been importing at great cost for years. The upstart artisan's audacious claim secured the patronage of King Henri IV (1589–1610), who arranged for workspace at the Louvre, then a cavernous royal residence.

Two decades later, in 1627, Louis XIII founded the Savonnerie carpet factory, granting royal privilege to Dupont and his apprentice, Simon Lourdet (d. 1671), who opened a satellite atelier in a former soap factory (*savonnerie*) on the Quai de Chaillot, on Paris's Right Bank. After the pair quarreled and parted, Dupont worked mainly from his *atelier* in the Louvre. Still, the fine wool carpets from both *manufactories* became known as Savonneries, whether woven by Dupont or Lourdet.

The process of creating a grand carpet with an immense, often allegorical, design was anything but simple or swift. An artist first methodically plotted a distinctive pattern, characteristically a symmetrical botanical motif or a neoclassical medallion against a blue-black background. The template, or "cartoon," as it was called, was then used as a guide for weaving the finished carpet on an upright loom, much like those used for making tapestries. To confirm that a weaver's painstaking work corresponded to the proposed design, mirrors were employed. So all-consuming was the process that included hand tying thousand of knots (some 90 symmetrical knots to the square inch) that historians report every carpet woven in the seventeenth century was for the king, either intended for a royal residence or for visiting dignitaries as state gifts. Records and documents also indicate that fewer than fifty Savonneries were woven throughout the entire eighteenth century.

Befitting the French decorative arts, the styles of the Savonneries evolved with the reign of each king. During the lengthy, lavish sovereignty of Louis XIV (1643–1715)—an era long considered the golden age for all artisans, the Sun King commissioned nearly a hundred Savonneries, each measuring no less than thirty feet, to cover the floor of the Grande Galerie in the Louvre. The project occupied the weavers for two decades; yet, the carpets were never used. Examples preserved in the permanent collections of the Louvre and the Metropolitan Museum of Art are characterized by elaborate decorative designs with complex themes pulled from Greek and Roman mythology, astronomy and the four elements—earth, air, water, and fire—on black ground. Yellows, limes and tans became preferred backdrops that complemented floral motifs and musical symbols as patterns shifted during the rococo reign of Louis XV (1715–74).

By the late-eighteenth century, however, less-costly reproductions of the Savonnerie were being produced by the rival carpet-making house of Aubusson—forever linked with an altogether different though equally intriguing carpet.

Early in the sixteenth century, Flemish weavers fleeing religious persecution settled in the French village of Aubusson, nestled in the Creuse Valley in Central France. In 1665, the Sun King granted the workshops there his royal patronage. It took another 115 years, however, before the Aubusson looms began producing what would become their signature artifact: low-warp, flat-woven floor tapestries created by hand on large-scale horizontal weaving looms.

Like the Savonnerie, the look of the Aubusson kept pace with the times. Early on, the intricate, elegant designs often channeled neoclassical themes, with extravagant garlands of naturalistic flora poised against a pastel background. Chinoiserie patterns also flourished in the eighteenth century. Similar to Savonneries, Aubussons were constructed of naturally dyed wool, meaning the tightly woven carpets proved extremely durable. Around the time of the industrial revolution (1815–48), Aubusson became the preferred floor covering of the burgeoning bourgeoisie.

Today, authentic and pristine examples of Aubussons from the Regency, Directoire, Empire, Restoration and Second Empire periods and later frequently emerge at auctions on both sides of the Atlantic. Triumphant bidders can take a bit of *bonheur* in the fact that they will tread where royalty, aristocrats and captains of industry did in centuries past.

An area off the kitchen serves as a second dining room—or an ideal place to simply enjoy the view.

ON PAGE 68: A kitchen worthy of a professional chef offers a taste of France. The fireback over the range is old. In the sixteenth century, a thick, decorative cast-iron panel propped at the back of a hearth not only protected a wall from fire but also reflected heat into the room. White diamond granite is from Walker Zanger. Barstools are by Charles Pollack.

ON PAGE 69: A Portuguese dining table mixes with Louis XV–style chairs in a breakfast room where the pineapple serves as a symbol of hospitality, a tradition dating back to the colonial days. The chandelier is old, but the eighteenth-century, heavily carved walk-in limestone fireplace from R.F. Imports, Dallas, wins top honors.

Harold Leidner, Dallas landscape architect, used symmetry and low Granbury stone walls to define a runnel situated amidst large trees. Leading to the steps are antique bricks—turned on their sides and set in a true herringbone pattern.

OPPOSITE: Cascading ivy drapes a massive stone fountain imported from Italy by Le Louvre Antiques, Dallas.

A mix of companionable styles creates a warm presence. Panels bedecking walls are hand painted. The ottoman fabric is by Florio.

OPPOSITE: Rather than the common triangular or arched pediment, a Louis XV–style house designed by architect Richard Drummond Davis has a dormer and scrolls above the entry.

A nineteenth-century Oushak—acquired by Abrash Rugs, Dallas, from a British estate—artfully grounds a grand, sumptuously comfortable dining room. The hand-painted wall covering is by Gracie. Rose Tarlow chairs wear Rogers & Goffigon; the curtain fabric is from Florio.

Rose Tarlow twig chairs, wearing indoor-outdoor fabric from Delany & Long, invite casual dining, much like a Left Bank café. The torchère—candelabrum—and chargers are from Jan Barboglio, Dallas.

A Genoese rock crystal sconce graces walls upholstered in Great Plains fabric, while rock crystal obelisks from East & Orient Company, Dallas, look on. The eighteenth-century Louis XV commode is retrofitted with an old marble sink. The Dutch perfected the decorative technique of ornamental veneering in the sixteenth century, assembling shaped pieces of wood in a pattern flush with the surface. Shortly thereafter, Florence became renowned for its pictorial marquetry, or intarsiatura, as known in Italy. American Patrick Edwards was one of three marquetry students invited to participate in a five-month study program at the prestigious L'École Boulle in Paris. He now heads the American School of French Marquetry in San Diego.

OPPOSITE: Demilune, or half-circle, stools in the style of Louis XVI offer a place to set a jeweled Judith Leiber handbag or a bag from Chanel, Hermès or Prada. The small benches belonged to an heir of John Jacob Astor (1864–1912), the wealthy businessman who was among the more than 1,500 victims of the sinking of the Titanic on April 15, 1912.

Far from the servant's scullery in eras gone by, this open kitchen makes it easy to collaborate with the cook. Moustiers, in Provence, is the accepted birthplace of faïence (tin-glazed earthenware). And although Americans think of the rooster as a traditional French country motif, mostly because he is a national symbol, the best place to spot one in France is in a toile fabric.

A serene master bedroom boasts glorious fabrics and 100 percent Egyptian cotton bed linens trumpeting 1,020-thread count. Higher numbers are not the end-all, but they do translate to longer, thinner fibers, or staples, which when woven are extremely soft to the touch. At Versailles, only the personal linens of the king and queen were purchased; court linens were rented. The repoussé (a metalworking technique whereby malleable metal is shaped or ornamented from the reverse side) mirror above the fireplace is nineteenth-century Dutch. Neoclassical intaglio seals were reproduced from a collection owned by Monaco's Prince Albert. The early-nineteenth-century Chinese table next to the bed is rare; from Trappings, in Carmel, California.

In her boudoir at Versailles, Marie Antoinette received her friend and favorite portraitist, Élizabeth Louise Vigée Le Brun, her fashion advisers, her hairdresser and other close friends. Monogramming adds a tasteful touch to the vanity chair from the Cameron Collection.

OPPOSITE: Siding the bed is a Cameron Collection chair wearing Bennison Fabrics. Overhead is a nineteenth-century intaglio—a design cut from a surface, leaving a relief in reverse.

Italian Panache

"Open my heart, and you will see / Graved inside of it, 'Italy.'"

So proclaimed Robert Browning (1812–89), undeniably enthralled with the region that inspired him.

When the celebrated Victorian poet died, *Ca' Rezzonico*, his *palazzo* (palace, literally) on the Grand Canal was bequeathed to his son. Today, it is the city-owned *Museo del Settecento Veneziano*, or Museum of Eighteenth-Century Venice, and the façade of the building bears his reverential tribute to Italy. And though Robert Browning was laid to rest in Poets' Corner of Westminster Abbey rather than on his beloved peninsula, a trace of the land that so entranced his soul is near, for the tombstone at his gravesite is chiseled from Italian marble.

Striking dramatic tones are a Steinway grand piano, an equally grand mandolin and a harp—all antiques. Among the aristocracy, classical music was key to the eighteenth-century art of gracious living. Marie Antoinette spent afternoons taking piano lessons at the now Hôtel de Crillon, overlooking the Place de la Concorde where she would later be publicly executed. In the calm of the Petit Trianon—her private domain away from the pomposity and glitter of Versailles—she also practiced the harp daily, inspiring other fashionable women of the period to do so too. The antique mirror is French.

More than a century later, however, it is not only the English poet and playwright who is captivated by the country; a global clique has also fallen prey to its charms. But Italy's breathtaking beauty alone does not inspire such gushing any more than its celebrated cultural institutions, tony hotels or Michelin-starred restaurants. Famed as these are, the magnetism of the boot-shaped peninsula runs much deeper. Enrapturing an international roster of admirers is the exhilarating attitude of a people whose innate warmth, admirable panache and passion for *la dolce vita* dates back to when Italy was the undisputed arbiter of taste and style.

In truth, Italy's allure makes it easy to forget its tangled history of invasions by the Austrians, French and Spanish, who each left an imprint of their customs and ways of living after

An Italianate villa projects an authoritative air, in keeping with its surroundings. When built in 1915, the façade was nowhere near as tall. Yet the current owners had no need to go back to the drawing board when they wanted to add a second floor, since interim owners had discovered plans to do exactly that. The date on the construction drawings: August 1929. In October that same year, the stock market crashed—followed by the onset of the Depression, destroying the original owners' plans. Otherwise, in 1929 the villa would have looked as it appears today.

An appreciation for the old, the rare and the unexpected ultimately led a hand-chiseled Italian marble sink to this powder room. Subtly nicked surfaces bestow character on Venetian plaster walls. The Italian side table is from The Mews, Dallas, and the chair from a local estate sale.

OPPOSITE: *Verre églomisé—as reverse painting on glass is called —insets adorn doors in the entry. Adding further visual impact are hand-painted walls banded in metallic gold then glazed—the work of Fort Worth, Texas, artisan JoAnna Lancaster. Limestone slabs form the pale stone floor.*

claiming this land as their own. Milan and Florence, for example, fell under the rule of France, while Sicily and Naples were ruled by Spain. Until the nineteenth century, Austria controlled Venice. From a network of duchies—territories ruled by dukes and duchesses—principalities and independent city-states, the Republic of Italy was created on March 17, 1861, with Turin as the capital. For political reasons, the center of government was moved to Florence in 1866, and finally to Rome in 1871, a year after being conquered.

Distinct regional styles had emerged during the Middle Ages (1000–1450) after the Romans had destroyed much of Italy's earlier Etruscan culture, whose exquisite gold and bronze metalwork was influenced by the Greeks. The Romans, too, borrowed elements from the Greeks; however, it was their own effective technological advances and skillful engineering that made possible spanning spaces with arched corridors, vaulted ceilings and rounded domes. Since then, their influence in Europe and the West has remained indisputable.

John Notman, who emigrated from Scotland in 1831, is universally credited with introducing the Italianate villa to the United States. In 1839, he designed Riverside, a private residence in Burlington, New Jersey. To the dismay of historic preservationists, it was razed in 1961. (Nearby, however, the much-photographed Prospect mansion built in 1851 at the center of Princeton's campus, stands in testament to the architect's well-documented love for Italy.)

Italian tile from Ann Sacks Tile & Stone is not about to be overshadowed by vintage Fortuny covering the chair.

OPPOSITE: *An antique nightstand with mirrored top sides a bed—glazed light green—that, too, is old.*

A chair in the style of Louis XVI holds monogrammed towels, while Louis XV stools insure even a young child can reach the sink. The hand-painted commode is old.

OPPOSITE: *Without compromising on comfort, a pair of antique mirrors dresses up a bedroom. Chandelier and bed also are old.*

For decades, Italy's strict laws have made it difficult to raze, renovate or even restore a residence deemed to be of historical significance. That might be changing, however, as evidence suggests local preservationists have fought more than a few losing battles lately.

Never mind that inheriting a palatial *palazzo* that has been in one's family for centuries may be a gift worth celebrating. Unlike antique furniture and vintage accessories, a *palazzo* is not necessarily a sustainable luxury. In fact, saving it from ruin can be an ongoing challenge. When hefty maintenance bills, to say nothing of the need to confront various states of disrepair, begin impinging on a modern-day lifestyle, even the most appreciative heir can balk at following in ancestral footsteps down chilly halls and traipsing across demanding grounds.

Not surprisingly, a number of heirs have plotted and then lobbied successfully in opposition of the country's rigorous preservation standards, something that once would have been unimaginable. Regardless that the façade of the building must retain much of its original outward appearance or that there are other limits to what one can and cannot do, converting the family *palazzo* into intimate apartments, it turns out, has become increasingly common in the past several years.

Fashionably appointed in fabrics from The Silk Trading Co., a master bedroom reads much like Milan. Reportedly, however, family studies experts say it will soon be inappropriate, even condescending, to call a bedroom the master, since women are buying and helping purchase more and more homes.

Doors open from the breakfast room onto a loggia—framed in arches—where family and friends gather to dine al fresco. Weather-resistant fabrics deck the sitting area. In Italy, most Tuscan-style homes include a loggia or portico framed by walls that once served as defense from attack.

99

A network of sprawling, airy rooms and narrow hallways revolve around a central enclosed courtyard of an Italianate villa. Mission Iron, in San Marcos, California, furnished the hand-forged iron door.

OPPOSITE: Arches frame a villa hall graced with a collection of antique crosses that once blessed Italy's various crops. The richly decorated early-seventeenth-century painted cassone—hinged chest that likely housed a bride's linens—belonged to the wealthy Medici family, who were highly influential in Florence from the fifteenth through the eighteenth century. With the Vatican in its midst, approximately 90 percent of Italy's 58 million people identify with Catholicism. And though only about one-third attend church regularly, religious symbols are common sights in most residences.

Amid the enduring, sumptuous stone *palazzi* at peace with their surroundings are *case coloniche*—modest farmhouses steeped in easy charm—stately villas with unassuming elegance and classical Venetian townhouses. In the midst of such plenty are the landscapes that inspired Renaissance artists Leonardo da Vinci, Raphael and, of course, Michelangelo, framed by *allées* of centuries-old cypress trees, olive groves and vineyards bursting with grapes.

In each of Italy's twenty regions thrives distinctive character and appeal, stemming from the customs, climate and terrain. These days, however, centrally huddled Umbria and Tuscany—once a thriving banking and silk center—share more similarities than differences. Together they have given life to a point of view with loyal local following and expanding global influence known simply as provincial Italian style or Italian country, befitting casual, family-orientated lives.

Naturally, settings come in many guises, from barely meriting a glance to appearing a bit much for modern times to deserving of special recognition—the latter being most noteworthy, of course. But whether Florence's dramatic Duomo, Rome's Pantheon or a sprawling hill town is the backdrop for an unhurried way of living, chicly rendered interiors radiate a passion for beauty, an intuitive sense of scale, harmony of color, and reflection of one's inner spirit. Those that outshine the rest are warm, unassuming, expressive and most importantly, inviting. To their credit, each has its own easy way

A veranda in Rancho Santa Fe, California, is the perfect gathering spot for al fresco luncheons. Reclaimed wooden beams and weathered limestone floors add rhythm to the façade.

of welcoming the steady flow of relatives and close friends central to life and encouraging them to linger.

Regardless that Italy has countless places to dine—some pricey but also a wealth of reasonable *ristoranti* and even less-expensive small *trattorie* (taverns), not to mention unpretentious *osterie* (wine bars) in busy neighborhoods that lend themselves to people watching—in a departure from American ways, stopping by each other's homes is practically a daily ritual, not only to share leisurely meals but also for the sole purpose of doing nothing more than relaxing. Preserving the tradition of *dolce far niente,* or sweet idleness, is a practice that most Italians have readily mastered as a way of reinforcing family ties and fostering relationships with an inner circle of friends.

Though interests and tastes differ, richly textured fine fabrics woven in surrounding mills that still use some eighteenth-century techniques mingle with approachable flair. Meaningful ancestral portraits, family photos in vintage frames and libraries of prized leather-bound books add interest. Marrying old-world artisanship with a mix of treasures amassed over time assures that homes look as if they've been furnished at an unhurried pace by several generations of family who had explicit ideas on style.

Emulating an indoor family living area, a space on the veranda is comfortably arranged in a similar way. It is but one of various informal outdoor spaces on the property.

As it is, there are no fixed design rules. That rules do not fare well in Italy is hardly a secret. Instead, most Italians favor an individualistic approach, letting innate feelings about what works personally shape the moods of rooms. Finding boundless inspiration in their surroundings—the country's art, architecture, land and seas—people carve their own identities, opting for purposeful touches suited to their needs and the way they want to live.

Drawing on tradition, finely crafted antique furniture—commodes, shapely secretaries and chairs with flattering silhouettes—that survived one crisis then another exudes enviable links loyal to the culture, while endless spiritual artifacts inevitably suggest religious preferences. Chandeliers worthy of the country's artisans flicker in hand-carved mirrors, some hung opposite one another, giving even small quarters more presence. In keeping with an aversion to heavy, ostentatious window treatments, curtains flow freely, with minimum fuss. Memorably patterned stone floors, meanwhile, bask in one another's reflected glow, rarely spoiled by rugs. North of Rome, faded terra-cotta (*cotta*) tile is popular. To the south, high-gloss glazed ceramic tiles are more fashionable; marble, indigenous to the country, is common in villas that are the epitome of Italian chic.

Faithful to their heritage, antique tapestries meander through halls replete with tiers of centuries-old paintings, some in need of cleaning. But these days, there is little doubt that rooms get much of their persona from diversely styled furnishings, handed down from caring ancestors who lived eras apart. It is as if confirming what Americans have known all along: being the favorite has its privileges, unlike in landed English families

Antique Italian ceiling tiles served as inspiration for the tile work by California artist Irene de Watteville above the Thermador range. Lush fresh produce in this trophy kitchen is from the famed Chino Farm in Rancho Santa Fe, California, which attracts not only those who live nearby but top-notch chefs from afar.

where first-born sons acquire all in keeping with the practice of primogeniture. (In France, possessions are divided equally among offspring, thanks to the Napoleonic Code of 1804.)

While next of kin may vie for a desk with a lengthy tale accompanying it—exaggerated or not—covet a mosaic-topped table or yearn for a commode, in reality, not everyone is lucky enough to inherit a wood piece hand painted in Venice any more than an armoire that belonged to *nonna's nonna*. As a result, living spaces are generally simply and pleasingly furnished rather than over decorated, and almost without exception, shy of pretension. Quite simply, in Italy, it seems, affectation has no place. Nor does clutter, intruding on floor space or anywhere else.

True to tradition, comfort abounds, meaning artistic merit does not take precedence over indulging family or pampering friends. In keeping with easy attitudes, there are always tables beside chairs for a glass of wine and plate of cheese; pillows to relax against; soft, clinging shawls to gather for added warmth and table and floor lamps placed just so for ending the day with *La Repubblica* or another of Italy's well-known daily papers (thus, shedding light on the notion that brighter is better except when entertaining, when lighting is kept low deliberately). There is even a chair next to the bathtub for stacking towels, placing a robe or relaxing while the tub fills.

Although the commonplace has never received the universal admiration of more important Italian pieces, the deft layering of

This door raises the traditional doggie door to a completely different level.

OPPOSITE: *At home in Rancho Santa Fe are three champion English bulldogs—all with villa privileges and all most personable. Left to right: Callis, Miss T and Thirst N. Howl.*

Much like in the farmhouses of Umbria and Tuscany, slatted shutters open into the room, framing a deep-set window.

ABOVE: *Bedskirt detail.*

OPPOSITE: *In fifteenth-century Italy, rich fabrics falling from a crown suspended over the bed were the epitome of luxury. Creating up-to-date splendor are fabrics from the Italian house of Dedar and textiles by Zoffany, KFI, and Dorian Bahr. The trunk at the foot of the bed is antique.*

conventional with chic makes stylish living look effortless, which is no small feat. As it is, stately andirons, fire screens, antique altar sticks and priceless clocks project an air of authority, while plants and bountiful bouquets, smartly arranged, plump settings with scenery for handling the cares, concerns and aspirations of everyday life.

Without fail, or the steep prices of the antiques-filled Le Sirenuse and other luxury hotels perched on the thirty-mile stretch of Amalfi Coast, bedrooms are sumptuously turned out. Impeccably pressed fine linens stretch across beds, hinting of romance. Down-filled bolsters sprawl beneath soft down pillows as feather beds snuggle against mattresses. Modest box springs appear tightly wrapped in blanket covers, shielded from prying eyes.

To be sure, filling empty rooms with shiny new furnishings is not something Italians understand. In fact, their way of thinking is much like those French who feel it is unpardonable to live in a house full of rootless pieces without any mystique or sentiment attached. Furnishings must be as meaningful as they are decorative, touting the mysterious bruises of history that led to the Italian way of life.

The Fortuny Mystique

Fortuny wing samples.

With the acumen of a scientist and the eye of an Old Master, Mariano Fortuny y Madrazo (1871–1949), a Spaniard who immigrated to Venice at the *fin de siècle*, earned his well-deserved reputation as a leading artistic figure of the Gilded Age. To this day, meticulously created Fortuny fabrics—using the techniques its originator perfected nearly a century ago—have managed to retain all the luster, prestige and awe-inspiring elegance that first captivated the upper classes on the eve of World War II.

To say that Mariano Fortuny set the standard for fine printed silks, cottons, and linens hardly conveys the scope or scale of his achievements. As the quintessential Renaissance man, he not only designed and produced a groundbreaking collection of textiles in the early 1900s, but he also achieved widespread recognition as a proficient painter, couturier, photographer and lighting engineer, ultimately securing more than twenty patents between 1901 and 1934. Despite the glory and veneration he received throughout his lifetime, this former student of French sculptor Auguste Rodin (1840–1917) and longtime confidant of writer Marcel Proust (1871–1922) likely never imagined the cachet that his fabrics would continue to command more than a half-century after his death.

As befitting an accomplished intellectual in the humanities, arts and sciences, Fortuny channeled global traditions and historical references to create the designs of his sumptuous fabrics. While basing his evocatively named patterns—"Olimpia," "Lucrezia," "Mazzarino," "Orsini"—primarily on Renaissance, Byzantine and Art Nouveau motifs, he also found inspiration from other cultures. Japanese kimonos, stenciled Celtic velvets and ancient Greek, Persian and Moroccan motifs, influenced his work.

Initially, Fortuny worked within his *palazzo*, Pesaro degli Orfei, experimenting tirelessly with both pigments and light until the way light danced over a fabric swatch was anything but happenstance. When he required a larger space to house the textile machines he invented, he purchased land on the Venetian island of Giudecca, building a factory to his precise specifications that opened in 1922.

Then, as now, the workroom that bore the Fortuny name employed only natural vegetable dyes, which is to say that dye lots varied. Although tonal variations were at times almost imperceptible, the designer often directed that rolls of fabric run through the presses more than a dozen times until the desired layering of hues had been achieved. To this day, retouching is still done by hand, *metro by metro*. Yet, for a century, mystery has shrouded the exquisite hand-printing techniques used in the designer's workroom. During his lifetime, he somehow managed to keep them to himself. We now know only that his still secretive methods cannot be rushed.

Thanks to the efforts of the late Contessa Elsie Lee Gozzi, production of Fortuny fabrics continues, using the same process and machinery developed nearly a hundred years ago. In 1927, the American interior decorator was "mesmerized" by the beauty of the textiles after seeing them in Paris and traveled to Venice to meet the artist. She soon became his confidante and sole United States distributor, discreetly passing on Fortuny's unique procedures in turn.

Though the factory remains in its original Venetian locale, the company's headquarters moved to New York City in 1988. At present, Fortuny patterns are hand printed on cotton only; yet, his radiant designs with signature metallic pigments still resemble brocade. Currently, the venerable firm boasts hundreds of different designs and colorways that all owe their genesis to a gifted man with an abiding passion for beauty in fabric form and a mystique all his own.

Venice may be slowly sinking and its population dwindling, but that has not dampened anyone's love for the sea-locked city with its maze of alleyways and iconic gondolas, canals and pigeons. According to the local tourist board, 6 million tourists spend the night each year and 15 million more day-trippers visit. There are no statistics on how many people have sought inspiration in Italy since the days of the Grand Tour. Pictured is Doge's Palace.

OPPOSITE: *Steps lead to an Italianate villa in La Jolla, California.*

In a culturally rich living room, washed chenille covers a sofa, while fabric from the German house of Gisbert Rentmeister wraps chairs. The cassone—an Italian wedding chest—is seventeenth-century. The eighteenth-century armoire is from the Piedmont region of Italy.

In a Tuscan cucina, (kitchen) with all the latest accoutrements, including a Sub-Zero glass-fronted refrigerator-freezer, a shapely hood takes center stage.

OPPOSITE: Chairs in embossed leather—an early pattern the French government approved for reproduction by Editions d' Art de Rambouillet, now distributed in the U.S. by Old World Weavers—surround a table by Michael Taylor. Interest in churches and monasteries led the homeowner to commission the painting by Carlsbad artist Jennifer Chapman. The setting is reminiscent of the imposing fifteenth-century Church of San Fortunato in Umbria. Dom Pérignon, a Benedictine monk, achieved more than a measure of fame by developing a method of preserving effervescence in wine, thus producing the sparkling wine we know as Champagne, named for the region.

The cozy breakfast area on the facing page takes a worldly view of Spain. Why Spain in an Italian kitchen? The shape of the space above the table was more hospitable to the former.

OPPOSITE: Lulu had absolutely no complaints about life at the SPCA, but the VIP treatment she now receives is even more to her liking. Besides, she can look out into the garden.

Exactly four centuries after the founding of Jamestown, word is that once a home's mortgage was paid in full, it was an early American tradition to cap the heavy upright post at the end of a handrail on a stairway with something grand. The large acorn-shaped newel post is French crystal and bronze. The one resembling a pinecone is English flint glass. Both are nineteenth-century, while the third is American, a brilliant cut glass, circa 1915.

OPPOSITE: "Piccolo Palazzo"— so named by the United States Ambassador to Italy—exudes noble taste. Particularly striking are the gouaches, circa 1730, from the Tuscany region. Also eighteenth-century is the marquetry chest. Opposite a pair of seventeenth-century Italian Renaissance chairs sits a nineteenth-century Biedermeier chair with zebra print. From the same period is the Serapi, a rug from Northwest Iran—an area known for its bold geometric designs and medallions. All are from The McNally Company Antiques, Rancho Santa Fe, California.

Elsewhere in the living room, a collection of spheres adorns a side table. A nineteenth-century bronze-and-ormolu sculpture of a monkey holds a rock crystal sphere. The large bubbled one is Italian Murano glass, circa 1950; the smaller sphere is English, dated 1900.

All the classic elements plus some inventive ones—that look as if transported from an antiques shop in Italy—warm a kitchen.

OPPOSITE: *An outdoor setting backs to a green belt and a stream. The prop on the far right once stood in Bonwit Teller, the New York department store founded in 1895 that catered to the Fifth Avenue carriage trade.*

Venetian Mirrors

The earliest mirrors were of highly polished metal, though occasionally the Romans made them of glass. By the fifteenth century, Germany produced glass mirrors most splendidly, though they all were convex. Then at the dawn of the sixteenth century, highly skilled artisans on the Venetian island of Murano perfected a revolutionary new procedure for making mirrors. Unlike those made in Germany, the ones they fashioned were flat.

So closely guarded was the process of blowing glass into cylindrical form, cutting it longitudinally and then placing it in a heated chamber where it was flattened with a wooden tool before being backed with an amalgam of mercury and tin, that mirror makers, or *artigiani di specchi*, were required to petition for official permission before leaving the small isle. This was intended to be a deterrent against industrial espionage from rival glass houses in France, Germany, England, the Netherlands and Flanders.

Assassins hunted fugitive glassmakers who left Murano without authorization. A renegade artisan named Paoli reportedly managed to travel as far north as the Normandy region of France, where his daughter discovered his lifeless body. Whether driving home a lesson or offering a fresh reminder, scrawled on a scrap of paper attached to the dagger through his heart was a single word: traitor.

Venetian mirrors were considered among the foremost symbols of power and prestige in the fifteenth, sixteenth and seventeenth centuries. At first, only royalty and nobility could afford these exquisite works of art. And little wonder: a two-foot-by-four-foot mirror in a silver frame, from the estate of the French finance minister Jean-Baptist Colbert, was appraised in 1693 at three times the value of a painting by Raphael. Yet, a century earlier, Italian-born Catherine de' Medici (1519–89) had 119 Venetian mirrors inset directly into wood paneling in her Paris *appartement*, setting new standards for extravagance as ruling queen following the death of her husband, King Henri II of France, in 1559. Inspired by the queen, her social peers emulated the look, prompting mirrored rooms to become the further rage—and assuring that they maintained their elitist status.

The Venetians held a near mirror monopoly until the late-seventeenth century. Then in 1678, Frenchman Bernard Perrot invented a way of making plate glass looking glasses with even smoother surfaces at Saint-Gobain Glass House in France, enabling production of mirrors unprecedented in size. Not known to shy away from minimalist thinking, Louis XIV quickly commissioned the mirrored gallery now known as the *Galerie des Glaces*, or Hall of Mirrors, at the Palace of Versailles. (In May 2007, the Hall of Mirrors reopened after a five-year renovation that restored the gallery to its former ornate splendor.)

There is no question that looking glasses varied in size and shape from the earliest days. Or that frames were fashioned from small mirrored pieces and borders, with intricate etching encasing nearly all. Among the most beloved and enduring motifs were delicate, ornate rosettes. Both the impeccable artisanship and surprising strength enabled myriad examples from early centuries to survive. Today, those with original glass are highly valuable. Whether adorning the walls of a museum or serving as the focal point of a room in a private residence, antique mirrors radiate unmistakable luxury compatible with their rich history and tantalizing legacy.

A powder room takes its cue from the bar in one of the world's most celebrated hotels, the Hotel Gritti Palace in Venice. Built in 1525, the splendid palazzo overlooks the Grand Canal and is a testament to verre èglomisè—an art form with painting on the reverse side of glass.

International Style

EVER SINCE THE EARLIEST SEAFARERS BEGAN navigating the Mediterranean trading grain and wine, the world's great waterways have played a pivotal role in connecting disparate cultures and peoples. The most intrepid explorers—the likes of Marco Polo, Amerigo Vespucci and Ferdinand Magellan—returned home from arduous voyages bearing a flood of exotic cargo that boosted living standards in Western Europe and in time made the world, as a whole, richer.

While France never dominated the high seas in the way that Spain and England did, she nonetheless managed a great feat: she ultimately reversed the tide, exploiting foreign trade to export her homegrown aesthetics until triumphantly becoming the world's largest exporter of luxury goods, with 36 percent of the global market, according to the April 19, 2007 issue of *The Economist*.

Taking indoor-outdoor living to a new level, a third-floor deck offers an idyllic spot to enjoy family, a wide circle of friends and sweeping views of the Gulf of Mexico. A lobster print from Clarence House dresses the settee and chairs. The Gauguin bar table is available to the trade from the David Sutherland Collection, Dallas.

The unfettered flow of merchandise and the sweeping influence of the French people continue unimpeded today, garnering international praise. For say what one will about the Republic's imposed maximum 35-hour workweek and high taxes, as tastemakers, the French reign supreme—a birthright we not only envy but also seek to emulate.

Unlike France, which for generations exported her own myriad styles, Italy's decorative arts were swayed by various cultures during decades of wars and breeched borders. Regardless that the Republic of Italy dates only to June 2, 1946, from the tip of the boot to the northern shores of Lake Como, a heightened sense of regional allegiance and pride of place resided deep in the Italian psyche that steadily gained force.

To be fair, other world centers of art and industry have also helped define design internationally and influence the way we

OPPOSITE: Humble painted chairs awash in coral dine in chic style on a balcony that is an extension of the living area. Back in the fourteenth century, Tuscan peasants hand shaped earthenware. Today, generously sized Italian pottery—such as Vietri's "Incanto" dinnerware, handcrafted to resemble lace and embroidery—is available at Neiman Marcus, Bergdorf Goodman and Barneys New York.

A sprawling vacation home on Florida's Gulf Coast is family friendly without sacrificing style.

OPPOSITE: *An Old World Weavers fabric aptly named "Tropic Bisque" surrounds a table perfect for dining en famille, as Création Baumann's lush, embroidered blossoms, cover a settee. (For centuries, the village of Pistoia, Italy, was the center of fine embroidery.) Floor lamps are by Palmer Designs, San Diego, embellished with Samuel & Sons glass trim. A mix of flowers fills William Yeoward vases, while Leslie Hannon's loop moss trim delivers the final touch to Nobilis curtains framing the view. Suiting relaxed living—a signature of this resort community as well as those that dot Italy's 36-mile fashionable stretch known as the Amalfi Coast—is dinnerware from Mariposa, Italy.*

The late legendary decorator Billy Baldwin advised, "Never forget that a room starts from the rug up." Less predictably, a napkin—happened upon at Amen Wardy Home in Aspen—suggested the color palette for this room.

now choose to live. The British Empire, for example, stretched from East Africa and India to Singapore and the idyllic Caribbean isles of Barbados, Jamaica, and St. Kitts during the reign of Victoria (1837–1901). By the 1910s, the Union Jack flew over nearly a quarter of the earth's population, with England's bustling import-export trade giving rise to lasting decorative styles, among them the Arts & Crafts and English cottage.

Sweden also emerged as a strong trendsetter. As Sweden's new ruler, King Gustav III (1771–92) was quick to indulge his passion for neoclassical design, having spent months at the court of Versailles. Within the first years of a reign cut short by his assassination, Gustav III ordered his palaces and country homes redecorated in numerous varieties of Louis XVI style, > 154

Once the province of smart dresses and blouses, bows, sparingly placed, now lend dash to two sofas and a settee without being overpowering. In eighteenth-century France, bespoke buttons adorned the finest upholstery. Considered small works of art, respected ébénistes (cabinetmakers) painstakingly hand carved some in wood, silversmiths engraved intricate designs in others and weavers specialized in creating others still in multicolored silk.

OPPOSITE: Reflecting the hues of the sea and sand, mirror-image sofas wear durable cotton, a Manuel Canovas stripe "railroaded" horizontally rather than in the traditional manner. Although the ancient Greeks voted by etching the name of their choice inside a shell, where their votes were impossible to erase, this clamshell appears more useful for chilling drinks. One can literally watch the tide roll in and out from vintage chairs in the style of Louis XVI flanking a painted table from Scully & Scully, New York City. Unseen is a banquette—French for upholstered bench—that provides extra seating.

In a coastal kitchen, lobster and crab are fitting staples. Original prints from Beaux Arts, Dallas, make a strong statement.

RIGHT: Designer's Guild lime green wall covering, Waterworks fittings and galvanized metal buckets from Crate & Barrel give a powder room added personality. Crab guest towels hand-embroidered in Madeira, Spain, are available through Sharon Blond Linens in Fairway, Kansas.

OPPOSITE: A kitchen gathers yet more stars when garnished with a soaring ceiling, marble countertops, sleek stainless steel cooking station and Le Creuset enameled cast-iron cookware from Williams-Sonoma.

In a setting that is the epitome of unassuming elegance, an antique chest from Parkhouse Antiques, Dallas, is one of a pair, as is the Brunschwig & Fils crystal lamp. A Clarence House check crowns the latter inside and out, for those who like to read in bed. Horizontal bands of chocolate brown and white stripes help establish the feeling of intimacy.

OPPOSITE: In island fashion, a cool white Pierre Frey matelassé—raised quilted design—splashed with seashells helps create a romantic getaway. Canopy bed is from Michael Shannon & Associates, San Francisco.

ABOVE: *With an enviable view across the dunes, a deck just steps from the sea is a tranquil spot for settling down with a good book—interrupted only by the sound of the waves. Fabric from Perennials wraps chairs.*

OPPOSITE: *In a serene suite, vintage chairs from Ceylon et Cie, Dallas, wear the same sumptuous matelassé as the bed on pages 138–139.*

ABOVE: *Suddenly the humble sea gull became the inspiration for the palette in His bathroom.*

LEFT: *Monogramming by Fern & Co., Dallas, adds to the luxury of towels by Matouk. Vendors these days are marketing the gram count of towels much as they have been promoting sheets with high thread counts. The higher the number per square meter, the heavier, fluffier and more absorbent the towel.*

In the Middle Ages, wealthy women housed their combs and ointments in a small cloth called a toilette. A special table fitted with drawers and compartments to store maquillage (make-up) made its debut during the reign of Louis XV. A Buccellati sterling silver tray and a Brunschwig & Fils crystal lamp with scalloped shade add a liberal dose of feminine charm to the dressing table. Fabric is by B. Berger. The vintage mirror is verre églomisé—or glass painted and gilded on the reverse side, a technique dating back 2,200 years to the Romans.

OPPOSITE: In a waterfront property stocked with all the accouterments of an upscale resort, there is every reason for the most personal of places to be distinctively feminine or masculine. Shown is Her bathroom. Rows of rhinestone buttons and trim add a bit of "bling" to a shapely vanity chair from the Cameron Collection. Across the way, an unseen terry shower curtain also drips in glitz—embellished with larger-than-life-size crystal teardrops meant to mimic falling raindrops.

Pierre Frey's peony pink highlights his rich dark chocolate on a sofa that invites conversation. A mix of humble trims, including one resembling malt balls, gives the window treatment a modern twist—courtesy of Straight Stitch. In a departure from the status quo, Ceil Johnson Custom Lamps lines shades inside, not just out, with a ribbon stripe by C. J. Dellatore. Both Straight Stitch and Ceil Johnson are Dallas based. The tables from the forties—a period long deemed an unpleasant reminder of World War II and the German occupation of France but now enjoying a renaissance—are from Jan Showers. Cabinet doors open to reveal a desk.

Bright, playful colors offer an invigorating break from the ordinary. Here, a vintage basket holds guest towels.

OPPOSITE: Bold tropical hues and resort comfort pack quarters with the ambience of the French islands, importing all the amenities a houseguest could possibly need: a tidily dressed bed with organic mattress, hand-pressed cotton sheets, a night table and reading light, drawer space, hanging space, bottled water and a plush robe. Print and stripe are from Sea Cloth, South Norwalk, Connecticut. Over the bed, in place of a grass hut ceiling, hangs a fabric canopy by Osborne & Little, Inc. Humble seagrass stretches across the floor, making itself at home. These days, Crocs, the rubber garden clogs, have a cult following in the United States.

A room evoking the Tropics needs a fitting tenant, such as this toucan from Beau Arts Gallery, Dallas. Throughout Europe, Sunday bird markets abound, selling both exotic tropical and common songbirds.

There's no chance of veering off course when a map—a classroom standard—offers the chance to explore all that the world has to offer. Jute bookends are in the shape of a "monkey's fist"—a type of sailing knot. Chest is old.

Inspiration can come from anywhere in the world, even less-than-grand places. In this case, a dock inspired a myriad of ideas.

OPPOSITE: Pierre Frey decks custom beds, while seaworthy Stark Carpet anchors the room. Modest woven baskets from Pottery Barn offer storage in tight quarters. The globe is from Barneys New York.

Porthole frames move from ship to shore as if preparing to weather a storm, while fabric from Ralph Lauren charts a clear course. The shower curtain's red also ribs Matouk towels.

OPPOSITE: *In a twist, white roping with bright red stitching gives a fresh edge to Roman shades floating from wooden rods and rings. Adding another splash of pizzazz is a painting by Gillian Bradshaw Smith, with clamps standing in for a frame. Appropriately, a buoy in Pierre Frey's "régate" or regatta, prompted the painting.*

with scores of gilded mirrors, cut-crystal chandeliers and laurel-wreath motifs embellishing ceilings and walls. The magnificent Pavilion of Gustav III, built in Stockholm as a retreat for the king and his family, nearly single-handedly became responsible for Sweden's reputation as the "Paris of the North,"—and still showcases lavish examples of eighteenth-century Gustavian furnishings.

But perhaps more important, artist Carl Larsson (1853–1919), a Swede from humble origins, indelibly refined and defined what would become his country's clean, tranquil aesthetic. Drawing inspiration from both English Arts and Crafts and Art > 161

OPPOSITE: *The water's edge is a top spring-break destination, according to media reports.*

In high season, a sleeping porch becomes the ideal place to stack grade schoolers. Also, it happens to be the perfect spot to play games on rainy days or once the sun goes down. Polka dot bedding is from Garnet Hill catalog.

A beach house calls for cool looks, meaning cheerful colors, playful patterns and photos of memorable moments lining the walls. Proving that practical can also be pretty, a stain-resistant cabana stripe from Lee Jofa stands up to waves of popsicles, snow cones and vanilla ice cream dipped in chocolate. Splashes of Glant ocean blue liquid wall covering also help keep worries at bay. Eco-chic ottomans are from Palecek in Richmond, California; the striped area rug is by Stark Carpet. The Brave Brown Bag—a book, shopping and beach essential—is the creation of Ontario, Canada, designer Charlotte McKeough.

BELOW: Stairs flaunt a bold pink and white awning stripe from Lee Jofa, artfully embellished with glass trim from Ellen S. Holt, Dallas.

Adding to the spirit of a vacation house, a spiffed-up vintage cupboard—once considered gloomy—keeps goggles and flip flops handy as if knowing that searching high and low for gear is far from fun. Bead board sheaths walls, offering protection from dampness.

OPPOSITE: Even though seeing doesn't necessarily mean believing, trompe l'oeil snow cones, smoothies and candy delight the hearts of those riding this beach butler. Decorative artist Gillian Bradshaw Smith purposefully turned a simplistic elevator into high art.

Nouveau traditions, Larsson pioneered new ideas that resonated on both sides of the Atlantic. To brighten interiors in a country with famously long winters and grim light much of the year, he and his wife, Karin, a textile designer, anchored spaces with quiet whites, delicate creams and watery blues, using as accents soft yellows, subtle pinks, misty grays, sage greens—and periodic glimmers of gold and bolder blues. Mirrors in painted, carved wooden frames multiplied available light, while striking tone-on-tone stenciling gave furnishings and walls a fresh identity without employing an extravaganza of accessories.

Half a world away, centuries-old Chinese decorative traditions also shaped European styles as sophisticated silks and ceramic arts wound their way into the export trade. Legend has it that around 11,000 B.C., a Chinese princess discovered the secret of the silkworm while sipping tea in her garden. A plump, white cocoon dropped from the branch of a mulberry tree and splashed into her cup, where the shell slowly unfurled to reveal its gift—a strand of silk.

The Chinese managed to shroud the origins of this shiny filament until sometime during the Han Dynasty (206 B.C.–A.D. 200), when groves of mulberry trees began cropping up in faraway Italy and Spain. > 172

For those ardent about extraordinary views, only a gathering place overlooking the Pacific Ocean would suffice. This deck invites casual dining both day and night year-round.

Reportedly, the Empress Eugénie, Napoléon III's glamorous wife, adored lace and made it fashionable. The town of Calais, on the shores of the North Sea, is the lace capital of France, though Chantilly and Valenciennes are also famous centers. The curtain panels here are circa 1890.

OPPOSITE: In an industry that feeds on innovation, the kitchen hood and countertops are French limestone—banded in scenes cut from dessert plates inset in terra-cotta pavers. French harvest workers artfully formed in marble and colored glass mosaics encircle the backsplash. Molds once used for making flatware act as bookends. They were happened upon at the flea market in the Provençal town of L'Isle-sur-la-Sorgue.

Lapped by the Mediterranean, Ionian and Adriatic seas, Italy's almost 5,000 miles of coastline offers endless inspiration. Among the country's most beautiful seaside resorts is Portofino. But Capri has also seduced everyone from Roman emperors to globetrotting Americans with its abundant natural beauty. Little wonder, then, that homes in the United States frequently offer a modernized take on Capri's cliffside villas.

Growing children once perched on bar stools that slide up to the kitchen island. Each still bears the child's name and year of birth.

OPPOSITE: *An airy, open kitchen-breakfast-living area serves as the center of family life—with the breakfast room opening onto a courtyard and the family room opening onto a deck overlooking the Pacific Ocean. The boat chandelier is old.*

A bedroom is simplicity itself—
until a grown daughter returns home
for a visit. Then it comes to life.
Both iron beds are old. Bead board
walls work with seaside living.

Cool quarters ideal for three boys not quite ready to sail the high seas were inspired by French sailors. Antique baskets, also French, are perfect for stashing casual clothes. Floors are easy-care pine.

169

A copper porcelain bathtub, a generously sized shower and floor-to-ceiling limestone add more than a modicum of beauty to a master bathroom designed to handle over-stressed lives. French limestone is from Walker Zanger.

OPPOSITE: *An antique Portuguese bed, circa 1820, is flanked by hand-painted chests. The decorative design replicates exactly the pattern on a chest that once belonged to Wallis Simpson, the Duchess of Windsor and controversial wife of Prince Edward, Duke of Windsor. A Brunschwig & Fils toile inspired the painted ceiling.*

Soon thereafter, Athens, Bologna and other European cities established independent silk houses. The Italian city-states created luxurious textiles, including coveted silk velvets studded with metallic threads. In 1309, with the shift of the papal seat to the South of France, Italian silk workers migrated to Avignon, where fabrication continued long after the pope returned to Rome some sixty-eight years later.

The French silk industry reached its creative summit in the nineteenth century. Seeking to rejuvenate flagging factories, Napoléon I (1769–1821) placed massive orders for fabric that would eventually adorn his multiple royal residences. By then, Lyon had become the leading center of silk production in the country, turning out fabrics unrivaled in quality, artistry and utter sumptuousness.

Today, fine silk fabrics from various countries swathe upholstery and billow from iron rods. Nonetheless, China has given the world far more than the celebrated byproduct of a moth. For centuries, the country's blue-and-white porcelain has enchanted and intrigued the West. In the 1600s, France and Holland began aggressively importing these fine ceramics, and fewer than 100 years later, Dutch ships were transporting several million pieces of this almost translucent dishware homeward each year. > 184

OPPOSITE: *An edgy, show-stopping carved flower has a chance to show off when serving as the centerpiece of a massive stone-topped table. Meanwhile, antique chairs boast Great Plains slipcovers, in keeping with Swedish practicality.*

In a blend of periods and styles, an eighteenth-century buffet from the Bordeaux region of France and a silvered mirror from Sweden offer a strong presence. The latter is from Watkins Culver, Houston. As in France, Sunshine—the family dog—has a special spot in the dining room. (The poodle, incidentally, originated in Germany, not France, according to David Frei, on-air commentator of the Westminster Kennel Club's 131st Annual Dog Show.)

A serene palette, both soothing and stylish, creates the illusion of space with help from the Fortuny curtains. A silk from Rogers & Goffigon, Ltd., cloaks the daybed.

OPPOSITE: *Breaking from conformity, a trumeau propped vertically leans against a wall in place of the usual landscape painting. It is from Brian Stringer Antiques, Houston. The Louis XVI canapé and fauteuils (armchairs with open sides) in the style of Louis XV are from Bremermann Designs in New Orleans, the most Gallic of American cities.*

When there is a household to run, thank-you notes to dash off or simply telephone calls to return, never mind a pizza to order, it helps to have a command center that is not only organized but also stylish. An extra closet in the family room morphed into a snug oasis large enough to hold a desk.

OPPOSITE: A kitchen is clearly au courant—with a pair of industrial lights from Skelton St. John, Houston, polished statuary marble-covered island and, not least, transparent Ghost bar stools. The famed Parisian decorator Philippe Starck designed the latter for Kartell, drawing inspiration from a formal eighteenth-century French chair. Slipcovers are peasant cloth, a Travers linen.

In its former life, a vintage sheet swaddled a nun's bed in an abbey in France. Today it graces late-eighteenth-century neoclassical Gustavian chairs painted white. The pair—from Jane Moore Interior Designs, Houston—flanks an unassuming Louis XVI carved console from Tara Shaw, New Orleans. The entry floor is stenciled.

Purple, once the domain of kings, today is fit for a pretty princess. The same lavender linen print covering the settee is used on the window shades on the facing page. Drawings and invitations top a ruffled bulletin board.

OPPOSITE: *Leontine Linens, New Orleans, wait the day a little girl outgrows her crib. A crown adapted from an antique fragment of boiserie—a word that comes from the French bois, meaning "wood" or "forest"—sits above the custom bed. Bed hangings are weathered linen by Ralph Lauren.*

Monograms date back to the Middle Ages, but the fonts used today are anything but conventional.

OPPOSITE: *A young girl's love of pink grew into a look by repeating a subtle Raoul Textiles toile on a chair in the style of Louis XV and on an ottoman. The Swedish pine secrétaire à abattant—a drop-front desk and wood bin—is from the Gustavian period (1772–1809).*

A blend of influences warms this master bath. Doors leading to the bedroom are old.

OPPOSITE: Quiet hues and a mix of shapes and textures create a space both comfortable and stylish. Bench in the style of Louis XVI is old.

Westerners also came to crave lacquer ware, dating back to 7000 B.C. In fact, early in the twentieth century, these shiny resin bowls and trays became *de rigueur* in affluent homes. Hand-painted furniture and accessories from both China and Japan—especially large hinged screens with elaborately painted scenes—had become chic on the European Continent 200 years earlier, around the same time that bamboo captivated English furniture maker Thomas Chippendale.

Southeast Asia (including present-day Thailand, Malaysia, and Indonesia) offered everything from nubby silks and color-saturated batiks to woven objects made of abaca, pandan, vetiver, water hyacinth, and buri. Meanwhile, environmentally friendly reeds, grasses, and other plant derivatives became the resource for familiar furnishings not only bringing ethnic élan to settings but also seemingly doing their part to save the planet centuries before this responsibility became fashionable. > 189

OPPOSITE: *Smartly tailored Cameron Collection sofas and Aubusson throws fabricated from a blemished eighteenth-century tapestry are worthy of notice. The game table is by the Old Timber Table Company, Dallas. Wood chairs are from Las Palmas, Los Angeles. Taking the French dictum to heart, a collection of family photos stand together, as do a grouping of candlesticks, thus having a stronger impact than if scattered around the room.*

Though some Americans claim the formal dining room is disappearing, others insist a home is incomplete without one. Fine antiques supporting the architecture and light streaming through the window make this space irresistible.

Europeans prefer all bedrooms to be on the second floor, while Americans often want a suite on the ground floor. But taking our lead from abroad, no longer do we purchase furniture in matching sets. Promoting global sensibility and off-hand glamour are an Italianate painted bed—the "Friuli" from Patina—an antique Italian side table and an iron chandelier culled from Country French Interiors, Dallas. Fabrics are by Pindler & Pindler, Inc.

OPPOSITE: The kitchen has long been the symbolic heart of the home on both sides of the Atlantic. But in a bow to twenty-first century America, a gourmet kitchen spills into the adjacent open breakfast room, where a round table assures that everyone feels equally important. The nineteenth-century iron chandelier is from The Whimsey Shoppe, Dallas.

Whether inside or out, unexpected details add interest. Here, far from pretentious grates from the Victorian period—an era in English history defined by the reign of Queen Victoria (1837–1901), who served her country longer than any other monarch—have their own value, transporting style to an outdoor room equally suited for relaxing and entertaining.

OPPOSITE: *Giving a guest room an inviting, South of France feeling: A Carlton V story-telling toile, meaning "cloth" in French, an Adele Kerr iron bed and transferware. Long enchanting the West, millions of pieces of blue and white porcelain had shipped from China to Europe by the eighteenth century. Inspired, English potters developed a method of applying single-color designs using copperplate engraving to print on paper and then transferring the etching to pottery. In the process, Staffordshire, England became an important center of transferware.*

Equally exotic today are the artifacts of Morocco, the North African land bounded by the Mediterranean Sea and the Sahara Desert and inhabited by the Moors, Arabs, and Berbers.

The "sentinel of Africa" vigorously traded olive jars and other colorful pottery, embroidered cotton and linen, hand-tooled leather, and tapestry-like khilim rugs prized for their textures, vibrant hues and distinctive geometric patterns. Clearly, in many ways, now as then, the country remains indebted to her artisans: government figures reveal that nearly a fifth of the three million inhabitants of Morocco work in the production of crafts. > 196

A collection of late-nineteenth-century French plaster-and-horsehair decorative medallions gives a family living area instant character and panache. Joyce Horn Antiques, in Houston, found the sample molds in a factory in France. Antique iron garden jardinière is from Kay O'Toole Antiques, also in Houston. Both chairs wear fabric by Brentano, Inc.

LEFT: Going global ensures an entry garners the attention it deserves. From France comes a nineteenth-century trumeau—overmantel paneling with a mirror, painting or relief—that boasts both its original mirror and a tapestry "cartoon." A rare colored Bakhshaish carpet, circa 1880, is from Iran. And the eighteenth-century painted rococo corner cupboard is from Sweden.

OPPOSITE: Linking the breakfast room with the kitchen is a vintage French bibliothèque that works as well as it looks. Area rug is an antique Oushak.

Worth crossing an ocean for is the verre églomisé French Art Deco reverse-painted mirror, circa 1940, purchased in the South of France. Large apothecary jars with labels are from Neal & Co. Antiques. Those with stoppers are from the Gray Door, Houston.

OPPOSITE: A dining room needs comfortable chairs a bit deeper than typical, flowers that don't interfere with conversations and preferably a round table, so lords, ladies and ordinary mortals sit as equals, just as kings and knights did long ago—with no one feeling left out, or sitting below the salt, as King Arthur once said. The eighteenth-century painted brasserie panel is from Houston's Chateau Domingue; the enfilade—low Provençal buffet with series of doors—is from Joyce Horn Antiques, also in Houston. The Italian chandelier is from St. Gertrude Antiques, New Orleans.

The chic mirrored hanging cabinet with brass detailing is from the Paris flea market, while the antique table—retrofitted with a copper sink—was found at Round Top, a highly anticipated semiannual happening in Texas where many top U.S. dealers proudly display their wares.

OPPOSITE: In the classic French kitchen, old copper pots, pans and egg white bowls are within arm's reach. Here, both the backsplashes and vintage lanterns that once adorned a ship are copper, too. The egg white bowl is from W. Gardner Ltd. Antiques, Houston. The hand-painted limestone tiles are from Architectural Design Resources, also in Houston. Countertops are concrete. Surprisingly, when moving, the French usually take their appliances with them.

Today the trade routes of centuries ago are as wide as the skyways and waterways, sending waves through all facets of existence. And so it is, with France and Italy being the wellspring of our inspiration, that we cultivate a global view, creating posh, memorable interiors filled with persona and attitude that work for us as well as everyone we welcome into our lives.

Another view of the dining room on facing page.

OPPOSITE: *A dining room revels in fabrics from Cowtan & Tout, Brunschwig & Fils and Coraggio, three of the design world's most recognizable names. Similar glasses in several sizes, each for a specific beverage, first appeared during the reign of Louis XIV. However, not until approximately 1830 did groupings of drinkware appear at each place setting. Today America is a nation that reportedly prefers wine over cocktails.*

The Provençal village of Vallauris is well known for its colorful pottery, a specialty developed in the sixteenth century. Here, the charm of the verdant French countryside melds with the present day.

OPPOSITE: Never mind that composer Ludwig van Beethoven owned five legless pianos. This time around, a piano's legs take pride of place. Salvaged from a fire, the ones pictured serve as the base for a breakfast room table, opening our eyes to possibilities. A Lee Jofa linen dresses the surrounding chairs.

Prized antique leather-bound books grace a console table. Establishing a personal library at Versailles topped the priorities of sixteen-year-old Louis XVI upon becoming king. Today some 200 used-book dealers (bouquinistes) line the quay in Paris.

OPPOSITE: When a plain vanilla ceiling won't do, an early map of Texas can offer insight into the growth of America's 28th state. Savvy collectors look for maps in original condition, meaning without tears, stains, cropped margins or evidence that the copper in any greens have oxidized onto the back. In addition, they seek paper with a high rag content that feels rough to the touch rather than smooth and lacks shine.

Directory of Designers

Shannon Bowers
Shannon Bowers Designs
3631 Fairmount St., Ste. # 103
Dallas, TX 75219
Telephone 214.521.7800

Don Brady
Don Brady Design
1301 S. 2100 E.
Salt Lake City, UT 84108
Telephone 801.582.4300

Cathryn Chapman
Chapman Designs
7026 Old Katy Rd., Ste. # 163 A
Houston, TX 77024
Telephone 713.864.8622

Laura Lee Clark, ASID
Laura Lee Clark Interior Design
5930 Royal Lane, Ste. E # 261
Dallas, TX 75230
Telephone 214.265.7272

Holly Heath Lydick
H. H. Lydick Interiors
116 Rivercrest Dr.
Fort Worth, TX 76107
Telephone 214.675.8833

Linda McCormick
Studio Veneto
7427 Girard Ave.
La Jolla, CA 92037
Telephone 858.551.2782

Stephanie Moore, Allied ASID
Moore Design Group
2111 Clark St., Ste. A
Dallas, TX 75204
Telephone 214.651.7100

Constance Noah
Constance Noah Design
2019 Soledad Ave.
La Jolla, CA 92037
Telephone 858.459.7051

Betty Lou Phillips, ASID
Interiors by BLP
4278 Bordeaux Ave.
Dallas, TX 75205
Telephone 214.599.0191

Christina Phillips, ASID
CMP Designs
2710 Simondale Dr.
Fort Worth, TX 76109
Telephone 817.927.5210

Marilyn Phillips
Loren Interiors
1125 River Bend Dr.
Houston, TX 77063
Telephone 713.973.6475

Mary Lee Singer
Trappings
P.O. Box 3105
Carmel, CA 93921
Telephone 831.626.4500

Directory of Architects

Larry E. Boerder, A.I.A
Larry E. Boerder Architects
4514 Cole Ave., Ste. # 101
Dallas, TX 75205
Telephone 214.559.2285

Richard Drummond Davis
Richard Drummond Davis Architect
4310 Westside Dr., Ste. # H
Dallas, TX 75209
Telephone 214.521.8763

Don Edson, A.I.A.
Don Edson Architect Inc.
5752 Oberlin Dr., Ste. # 104
San Diego, CA 92121
Telephone 858.452.1860

Robbie Fusch
Fusch, Serold & Partners
5950 Berkshire Lane, Ste. # 1500
Dallas, TX 75225
Telephone 214.696.0152

Harold Leidner
Harold Leidner Landscape Architects
1601 Surveyor Blvd.
Carrollton, TX 75006
Telephone 972.418.5244

Scott Merrill, A.I.A.
Merrill, Pastor & Colgan Architects
929 Azalea Lane, Ste. # B
Vero Beach, FL 32963
Telephone 772.492.1983

Kenneth A. Newberry, A.I.A.
Newberry Campa Architects
708 E. 19th Ave.
Houston, TX 77008
Telephone 713.862.7992

Drew Patterson, A.I.A.
Tony Crisafi, A.I.A
Island Architects
7632 La Jolla, CA 92037
Telephone 858.459.9291

Randall Walton, A.I.A.
Walton & Walton Architecture
1407 Texas St., Ste. #104
Fort Worth, Texas 76102
Telephone 817.732.1536

Scott Watson
Watson Design
3116 W. 6th St.
Fort Worth, TX 76107
Telephone 817.882.8882

Although the U.S. real estate market has slowed markedly, the country's 2006 frenzy fueled a rash of tear-downs in 300 communities in 33 states, according to the National Trust for Historic Preservation in Chicago. With the influence of the French knowing no bounds, a Renaissance château designed by Dallas architect Larry E. Boerder will soon stand on this land. In French minds, urban sprawl is a constant danger.

Designer Photographic Credits

Shannon Bowers: 172, 173, 174, 175, 176, 177, 178, 179, 180–181, 182, 183

Don Brady: 160–161, 162, 163, 164, 165, 166–167, 168–169, 170, 171

Cathryn Chapman: 50, 51, 52–53, 54, 55, 56–57, 58, 59

Laura Lee Clark: 10–11, 13, 60, 61, 62, 63, 65, 68, 69, 70–71, 72, 73

Holly Heath Lydick: 8, 86–87, 88, 89, 90, 91, 92, 93, 94, 95, 96–97, 98–99

Linda McCormick: 116–117, 118, 119, 120, 121

Stephanie Moore: 196, 197, 198, 199, 200, 201, 207, 208

Constance Noah: Back Jacket, 100, 101, 103, 104, 107, 108, 109, 110, 111, 114, 122, 123, 124, 125, 127

Betty Lou Phillips: Front Jacket, Title Page, 14–15, 17, 18, 19, 20–21, 22, 23, 24–25, 26, 27, 28, 29, 30, 31, 32–33, 34–35, 36–37, 38–39, 40, 41, 42, 43, 44–45, 46, 47, 48, 49, 128–129, 130, 131, 132, 133, 134–135, 136, 137, 138–139, 140, 141, 142, 143, 144–145, 146, 147, 148–149, 150, 151, 152, 153, 154, 155, 156, 157, 158, 159, 202, 205

Christina Phillips: 184, 185, 186, 187, 188, 189

Marilyn Phillips: 6, 190, 191, 192, 193, 194, 195

Mary Lee Singer: Copyright Page, 74–75, 76, 77, 78, 79, 80–81, 82–83, 84, 85

Architect Photographic Credits

Larry E. Boerder: 202

Richard Drummond Davis: Copyright Page, 74–75, 76, 77, 78, 79, 80–81, 82–83, 84, 85

Don Edson: 160–161, 162, 163, 165, 166–167, 168–169, 170, 171

Robbie Fusch: 10–11, 13, 60, 61, 62, 63, 65, 68, 69, 70–71, 72, 73

Harold Leidner: 70–71, 73

Scott Merrill: 128–129, 130 , 131, 132, 134–135, 136, 137, 138–139, 140, 141, 142, 143, 144, 145, 146, 147, 148–149, 150, 151, 152, 153, 154, 156, 157, 158, 159, 205

Kenneth A. Newberry: 51, 52–53, 54, 55, 56–57, 58, 59

Drew Patterson and Tony Crisafi: Back Jacket, 100, 101, 103, 104, 107, 108, 109, 110, 111

Randall Walton: 8, 86–87, 88, 89, 90, 91, 92, 93, 94, 95, 96–97, 98–99

Scott Watson: 184, 185, 186, 187, 189

Photographic Credits

All images are by Dan Piassick except:

Betty Lou Phillips 115, 151, 163 (bottom), 202

Antique Furnishings and Accessories

Agostino Antiques, Ltd.
21 Broad St.
Red Bank, NJ 07701
Telephone 732.345.7301
agostinoantiques.com

Ambiance Antiques
135 Rhode Island St.
San Francisco, CA 94103
Telephone 415.255.9006
ambianceantiques.com

Annette Schatte Antiques
1928 Bissonnet St.
Houston, TX 77005
Telephone 713.524.0990

Anthony Antiques & Fine Arts
401 E. 200 S.
Salt Lake City, UT 84111
Telephone 801.328.2231

Area
5600 Kirby Dr.
Houston, TX 77005
Telephone 713.668.1668

Bremermann Designs
3943 Magazine St.
New Orleans, LA 70115
Telephone 504.891.7763
bremermanndesigns.com

Brian Stringer Antiques
2031 W. Alabama St.
Houston, TX 77006
Telephone 713.526.7380
brianstringersantiques.com

Carl Moore Antiques
1610 Bissonnet St.
Houston, TX 77005
Telephone 713.524.2502
carlmooreantiques.com

Charles Gaylord & Co.
Two Henry Adams St., Ste. 406
San Francisco, CA 94103
Telephone 415.861.6300
charlesgaylord.com

Château Domingue
3615-B W. Alabama St.
Houston, TX 77027
Telephone 713.961.3444
chateaudomingue.com

Country French Interiors
1428 Slocum St.
Dallas, TX 75207
Telephone 214.747.4700
countryfrenchinteriors.com

Décor de France
24 N. Blvd. of the Presidents
Sarasota, FL 34236
Telephone 941.388.1599
decoredefrance.com

Donald J. Embree Antiques
1115 Slocum St.
Dallas, TX 75207
Telephone 214.760.9141

Duane Antiques
176 Duane St.
New York, NY 10013
Telephone 212.625.8066
duaneantiques.com

East & Orient Company
1123 Slocum St.
Dallas, TX 75207
Telephone 214.741.1191
eastandorient.com

Ed Hardy San Francisco
188 Henry Adams St.
San Francisco, CA 94103
Telephone 415.626.6300
edhardysf.com

The French Hare, Ltd.
418 King St.
Charleston, SC 29403
Telephone 843.577.0451
thefrenchhare.com

The Gables
711 Miami Cr.
Atlanta, GA 30324
Telephone 800.753.3342
thegablesantiques.com

Galerie de France
184-186 Duane St.
New York, NY 10013
Telephone 212.965.0969

Gore Dean Antiques
2828 Pennsylvania Ave.
Washington, DC 20007
Telephone 202.625.1776
goredeanantiques.com

The Gray Door
1809 W. Gray St.
Houston, TX 77019
Telephone 713.521.9085

Inessa Stewart Antiques
5330 Bluebonnet Blvd.
Baton Rouge, LA 70809
Telephone 225.368.8600
inessa.com

Inessa Stewart Antiques
5201 W. Lovers Ln.
Dallas, TX 75209
Telephone 214.366.2660
inessa.com

Jacqueline Adams Antiques
2300 Peachtree Rd., Ste. B 110
Atlanta, GA 30309
Telephone 404.355.8123
jacquelineadamsantiques.com

Jacqueline Adams Antiques
The Galleries of Peachtree Hills
425 Peachtree Hills Ave.
Atlanta, GA 30305
Telephone 404.869.6790
jacquelineadamsantiques.com

Jane Moore Interiors
2922 Virginia St.
Houston, TX 77098
Telephone 713.526.6113

Jefferson West Inc.
9310 Jefferson Blvd.
Culver City, CA 90232
Telephone 310.558.3031
jeffersonwest.com

John Rosselli & Associates
523 E. 73rd St.
New York, NY 10021
Telephone 212.772.2137
johnroselliantiques.com

John Rosselli & Associates
255 E. 72nd St.
New York, NY 10021
Telephone 212.737.2252
johnrosselliantiques.com

Joseph Minton Antiques
1410 Slocum St.
Dallas, TX 75207
Telephone 214.744.3111
mintonantiques.com

Joyce Horn Antiques
1022 Wirt Rd., Ste. 326
Houston, TX 77055
Telephone 713.688.0507
joycehornantiques.com

KM Antiques of London
979 3rd Ave., Ste. 1702
New York, NY 10022
Telephone 212.888.7950

Le Louvre French Antiques
1400 Slocum St.
Dallas, TX 75207
Telephone 214.742.2605
lelouvre-antiques.com

Lee Stanton Antiques
769 N. La Cienega Blvd.
Los Angeles, CA 90069
Telephone 310.855.9800
leestanton.com

Lee Stanton Antiques
769 N. La Cienega Blvd.
Los Angeles, CA 90069
Telephone 310.855.9800
leestanton.com

Legacy Antiques
1406 Slocum St.
Dallas, TX 75207
Telephone 214.748.4606
legacyantiques.com

The Lotus Collection
445 Jackson St.
San Francisco, CA 94111
Telephone 415.398.8115
ktaylor-lotus.com

Lovers Lane Antique Market
5001 W. Lovers Ln.
Dallas, TX 75209
Telephone 214.351.5656
loverslaneantiques.com

Made In France
2912 Ferndale St.
Houston, TX 77098
Telephone 713.529.7949

Maison Felice
73-960 El Paseo
Palm Desert, CA 92260
Telephone 760.862.0021
maisonfelice.com

Mariette Himes Gomez
506 E. 74th St.
New York, NY 10021
Telephone 212.288.6856
gomezassociates.com

Marston Luce
1651 Wisconsin Ave., N.W.
Washington, DC 20007
Telephone 202.333.6800

Metropolitan Artifacts, Inc.
Architectural Antiques
4783 Peachtree Rd.
Atlanta, GA 30341
Telephone 770.986.0007
metropolitanartifacts.com

The Mews
1708 Market Center Blvd.
Dallas, TX 75207
Telephone 214.748.9070
themews.net

Neal & Co.
4502 Greenbriar St.
Houston, TX 77005
Telephone 713.942.9800

Newell Art Galleries, Inc.
425 E. 53rd St.
New York, NY 10022
Telephone 212.758.1970
newel.com

Niall Smith
306 E. 61st St.
New York, NY 10021
Telephone 212.750.3985

Nick Brock Antiques
2909 N. Henderson St.
Dallas, TX 75206
Telephone 214.828.0624

Orion Antique Importers, Inc.
1435 Slocum St.
Dallas, TX 75207
Telephone 214.748.1177
oriondallas.com

Parc Monceau, Ltd.
425 Peachtree Hills Ave., # 15
Atlanta, GA 30305
Telephone 404.467.8107
parcmonceauatl.com

Patina Atelier Antiques
3364 Sacramento St.
San Francisco, CA 94118
Telephone 415.409.2299

Pied-' A'- Terre
7645 Girard Ave.
La Jolla, CA 92037
Telephone 858.456.4433

Pittet & Co.
1215 Slocum St.
Dallas, TX 75207
Telephone 214.748.8999
pittet.com

Round Trip Imports
33071 W. 83rd St.
De Soto, KS 66018
Telephone 913.583.1511
roundtripimports.com

R.F. Imports
5950 Berkshire Ln., Ste. 1500
Dallas, TX 75225
Telephone 214.696.0152

Shabby Slip
3522 Magazine St.
New Orleans, LA 70115
Telephone 504.897.5477

Sidney Lerer
420 Richmond Ave.
Point Pleasant Beach, NJ 08741
Telephone 732.899.8949

Skelton St. John
2143 Westheimer Rd.
Houston, TX 77098
Telephone 713.524.1990

South of Market
345 Peachtree Hills Ave.
Atlanta, GA 30305
Telephone 404.995.9399
southofmarket.biz

St. Gertrude Antiques
3424 Magazine St.
New Orleans, LA 70015
Telephone 504.897.9258
stgertrude.com

The Stalls
116 Bennett St.
Atlanta, GA 30309
Telephone 404.352.4430
thestalls.com

The Whimsey Shoppe Slocum
1444 Oak Lawn Ave.
Dallas, TX 75207
Telephone 214.745.1800

Tara Shaw Antiques
1845-A W. Alabama
Houston, TX 77098
Telephone 713.533.9744

Therien & Co.
716. N. La Cienega Blvd.
Los Angeles, CA 90069
Telephone 310.657.4615
411 Vermont St.
San Francisco, CA 94103
Telephone 415.956.8850
therien.com

Uncommon Market, Inc.
2701-2707 Fairmount St.
Dallas, TX 75201
Telephone 214.871.2775

Vieux Carré
546 Hudson St.
New York, NY 10014
Telephone 212.647.7633

Watkins Culver
2308 Bissonnet St.
Houston, TX 77005
Telephone 713.529.0597

W. Gardner, Ltd.
2930 Ferndale
Houston, TX 77098
Telephone 713.521.1027
wgardnerltd.com

Tres Belle
2435 East Coast Hwy.
Corona Del Mar, CA 92625
Telephone 949.723.0022

Artisans

Brad Oldham, Inc.
1551 Edison St.
Dallas, TX 75207
Telephone 214.239.3993
bradoldham.com

Chuck Walter
511 S. Elm St.
Arlington, TX 76010
Telephone 817.229.9453

David Lyles
514 Summit Dr.
Richardson, TX 75081
Telephone 972.240.0051
seedavidlyles.com

EyeCon Studios
1341 Plowman
Dallas, TX 75203
Telephone 214.941.0500
eye-c.com

Fern & Co.
2732 Amherst Ave.
Dallas, TX 75225
Telephone 214.696.6337

Gillian Bradshaw Smith
311 N. Winnetka Ave.
Dallas, TX 75208
Telephone 214.948.8472

Irene de Watteville
749 N. Granados Ave.
Solana Beach, CA 92075
Telephone 858.755.0627

Jackie Musso
6530 St. Moritz
Dallas, TX 75214
Telephone 214.828.1249

Jennifer Chapman Designs
7049 Via Cabana
Carlsbad, CA 92009
Telephone 760.602.0079
jenniferchapmandesign.com

Irene de Watteville
749 N. Granados Ave.
Solana Beach, CA 92075
Telephone 858.755.0627

Joanna Otte Studios
6358 Waverly Way
Fort Worth, TX 76116
Telephone 817.235.8233

Jo Mattison
4100 San Carlos St.
Dallas, TX 75205
Telephone 214.521.9337

Kay Fox's Custom Creations
2404 Springpark Way
Richardson, TX 75082
Telephone 972.437.4227

Patrick Edwards
3815 Utah St.
San Diego, CA 92104
Telephone 619.298.0864

Bath Fittings

Czech & Speake
350 11th St.
Hoboken, NJ 07030
Telephone 800.632.4165
homeportfolio.com

Herbeau Creations of America
2725 Davis Blvd.
Naples, FL 34104
Telephone 800.547.1608
herbeau.com

Kallista, Inc.
2446 Verna Ct.
San Leandro, CA 94577
Telephone 888.4.Kallista
kallistainc.com

Sherle Wagner, International
300 E. 62nd St.
New York, NY 10022
Telephone 212.758.3300
sherlewagner.com

Sunrise Specialty
930 98th Ave.
Oakland, CA 94603
Telephone 510.729.7277
sunrisespecialty.com

Waterworks
60 Backus Ave.
Danbury, CT 06810
Telephone 800.899.6757
waterworks.com

Carpets

Abrash Rugs
1025 N. Stemmons Frwy., Ste. 760
Dallas, TX 75207
Telephone 214.573.6262
abrashrugs.com

Asmara, Inc.
88 Black Falcon Ave.
Boston, MA 02210
Telephone 800.451.7240
asmarainc.com

Beauvais Carpets
201 E. 57th St.
New York, NY 10022
Telephone 212.688.2265
beauvaiscarpets.com

Carol Piper Rugs, Inc.
1809 W. Gray St.
Houston, TX 77019
Telephone 713.524.2442
carolpiperrugs.com

Design Materials
241 S. 55th St.
Kansas City, KA 66106
Telephone 913.342.9796

Farzin Rugs & Design
955 Slocum St.
Dallas, TX 75207
Telephone 214.747.1511

Hokanson
Decorative Ctr.
5120 Woodway Rd.
Houston, TX 77056
Telephone 800.243.7771
hokansoncarpet.com

Mansour
8600 Melrose Ave.
Los Angeles, CA 90069
Telephone 310.652.9999

Mark, Inc.
323 Railroad Ave.
Greenwich, CT 06830
Telephone 203.861.0110
brunschwig.com

Nouri & Sons Antique Oriental Rugs
3845 Dunlavy St.
Houston, TX 77006
Telephone 713.523.6626
nouriantiquerugs.com

Surely nowhere is the impulse to spoil a loyal friend greater than in America. Fittingly then, Patina—with the necessary luxury cachet—introduces a sumptuous painted bed. And since a bed alone isn't quite enough, monogrammed linens add a personal touch. They are by Frette, the renowned Milan firm that bedecked sleeping cars on the famous Orient Express. The coverlet is Fortuny, naturellement. This is not to say that Jackson doesn't insist on jumping up on the author's bed!

Renaissance Collection
1532 Hi Line Dr.
Dallas, TX 75207
Telephone 214.698.1000
rencollection.com

Rosecore Carpet Co., Inc.
D&D Building
979 Third Ave.
New York, NY 10022
Telephone 212.421.7272
rosecore.com

Stark Carpet
D&D Building
979 Third Ave.
New York, NY 10022
Telephone 212.752.9000
starkcarpet.com

Stephen Miller Gallery
800 Santa Cruz Ave.
Menlo Park, CA 94025
Telephone 650.327.5040
stephenmillergallery.com

Decorative Hardware

E. R. Butler & Co., Inc.
Maison J. Vervloeot-Faces
75 Spring St., 5th Fl.
New York, NY 10012
Telephone 212.925.3565
erbutler.com

Nanz Custom Hardware
20 Vandam St.
New York, NY 10013
Telephone 212.367.7000
nanz.com

Palmer Designs
7875 Convoy Ct.
San Diego, CA 92111
Telephone 858.576.1350
palmer-design.com

P. E. Guerin, Inc.
21-23 Jane St.
New York, NY 10014
Telephone 212.243.5270
peguerin.com

Fabrics & Furniture

Anna French
108 Shakespeare Rd.
London, SE 0QW
Telephone 020.7737.6555
annafrench.co.uk

B. Berger Fabrics
1380 Highland Rd.
Macedonia, OH 44056
Telephone 330.425.3838
bberger.com

Beacon Hill
225 Foxboro Blvd.
Foxboro, MA 02035
Telephone 800.343.1470
beaconhilldesign.com

Bennison Fabrics, Inc.
76 Greene St.
New York, NY 10012
Telephone 212.941.1212
bennisonfabrics.com

Bergamo Fabrics, Inc.
D&D Building
979 Third Ave., 17th Fl.
New York, NY 10022
Telephone 212.888.3333
bergamofabrics.com

Boussac Fadini
15 E. 32nd St., 6th Fl.
New York, NY 10016
Telephone 212.213.3099

Brentano Inc.
1451 Paddock Dr.
Northbrook, IL 60062
Telephone 800.338.7210
brentanofabrics.com

Brunschwig & Fils, Inc.
75 Virginia Rd.
North White Plains, NY 10603
Telephone 914.684.5800
brunschwig.com

The Budji Collections, Inc.
7302 E. Helm Dr., Ste. 2002
Scottsdale, AZ 85260-3126
Telephone 480.905.3126
budji.com

The Cameron Collection
150 Dallas Design Center
1025 N. Stemmons Frwy.
Dallas, TX 75207
Telephone 214.744.1544

Carlton V, Ltd.
D&D Building
979 Third Ave., 15th Fl.
New York, NY 10022
Telephone 212.355.4525

Charles Pollock Reproductions, Inc.
6824 Lexington Ave.
Los Angeles, CA 90038
Telephone 323.962.0440
charlespollockrepro.com

Charles P. Rogers
55 W. 17th St.
New York, NY 10011
Telephone 212.675.4400
charlesprogers.com

Christopher Norman, Inc.
41 W. 25th St., 10th Floor
New York, NY 10010
Telephone 212.647.0303
christophernorman.com

Christopher Hyland, Inc.
979 3rd Ave., Ste. 1710
New York, NY 10022
Telephone 212.688.6121
christopherhyland.com

C. J. Dellatore
133 W. 25th St., Ste. 9W
New York, NY 10001
Telephone 212.352.0160

Clarence House, Inc.
211 E. 58th St.
New York, NY 10022
Telephone 800.221.4704
clarencehouse.com

Classic Revivals, Inc.
One Design Center Pl., Ste. 534
Boston, MA 02210
Telephone 617.574.9030

Coraggio Textiles
1750 132nd Ave., N.E.
Bellevue, WA 98005
Telephone 425.462.0035
coraggio.com

Cowtan & Tout
111 Eighth Ave., Ste. 930
New York, NY 10011
Telephone 212.647.6900

Delany & Long, Ltd.
41 Chestnut St.
Greenwich, CT 06830
Telephone 203.532.0010
delanyandlong.com

Dennis & Leen
8734 Melrose Ave.
Los Angeles, CA 90069
Telephone 310.652.0855

Donghia, Inc.
256 Washington St.
Mount Vernon, NY 10553
Telephone 914.662.2377
donghia.com

Elizabeth Dow, Ltd.
155 Sixth Ave., 4th Fl.
New York, NY 10013
Telephone 212.219.8822
edowltd.aol.com

Erika Brunson
15442 Ventura Blvd., Ste. 200
Sherman Oaks, CA 91403
Telephone 818.252.4947
erikabrunson.com

The Farmhouse Collection, Inc.
807 Russet St.
Twin Falls, ID 83301
Telephone 208.736.8700
farmhousecollection.com

The Florio Collection
8815 Dorrington Ave.
West Hollywood, CA 90048
Telephone 310.273.8003
floriocollection.com

Fortuny, Inc.
D&D Building
979 Third Ave., 16th Fl.
New York, NY 10022
Telephone 212.753.7153
fortuny.com

Gregorius/ Pineo
653 N. La Cienega Blvd.
Los Angeles, CA 90069
Telephone 310.659.0588

Hamilton, Inc.
8417 Melrose Pl.
Los Angeles, CA 90069
Telephone 323.655.9193

Henry Calvin Fabrics
2046 Lars Way
Medford, OR 97501
Telephone 541.732.1996
Telephone 888.732.1996 (toll-free)
henrycalvin.com

Hinson & Company
2735 Jackson Ave.
Long Island City, NY 11101
Telephone 718.482.1100

James Brindley of Harrogate
29-31 James St.
Harrogate, North Yorkshire HG1 1QY
Telephone 01423 560757
jamesbrindley.com

Jan Barboglio
145 Cole Ave.
Dallas, TX 75207
Telephone 214.698.1920

Jane Keltner
94 Cumberland Blvd.
Memphis, TN 38112
Telephone 800.487.8033
janekeltner.com

Jane Shelton
205 Catchings Ave.
Indianola, MS 38751
Telephone 800.530.7259
janeshelton.com

Jim Thompson
1694 Chantilly Dr.
Atlanta, GA 30324
Telephone 800.262.0336
jimthompson.com

J. Robert Scott
500 N. Oak St.
Inglewood, CA 90302
Telephone 310.680.4300
jrobertscott.com

Koplavitch & Zimmer Textiles
18600 Crenshaw Blvd.
Torrance, CA 90504
Telephone 866.447.5100
koplavitchandzimmer.com

Kravet Fabrics, Inc.
225 Central Ave. S.
Bethpage, NY 11714
Telephone 516.293.2000
kravet.com

La Lune Collection
930 E. Burleigh St.
Milwaukee, WI 53212
Telephone 414.263.5300
lalunecollection.com

Lee Jofa
225 Central Ave. So.
Bethpage, NY 11714
Telephone 888.LeeJofa
leejofa.com

Malabar Fabrics
8A Trowbridge Dr.
Bethel, CT 06801
Telephone 877.625.2227
malabar.co.uk

Manuel Canovas
111 Eighth Ave., Ste. 930
New York, NY 10011
Telephone 212.647.6900
manuelcanovas.com

Marvic Textiles, Ltd.
30-10 41st Ave., 2nd Fl.
Long Island City, NY 11101
Telephone 718.472.9715
marvictextiles.co.uk

Michael Taylor Designs
1500 Seventeenth St.
San Francisco, CA 94107
Telephone 415.558.9940
michaeltaylordesigns.com

Minton Spidell, Inc.
8467 Steller Dr.
Culver City, CA 90232
Telephone 310.836.0403

Mokum Textiles
98 Barcom Ave.
Rushcutters Bay NSW 2011
Telephone 1800 123 705
mokumtextiles.com

Nancy Corzine
256 W. Ivy Ave.
Inglewood, CA 90302
Telephone 310.672.6775

Niermann Weeks
Fine Arts Building
232 E. 59th St.
New York, NY 10022
Telephone 212.319.7979
niermannweeks.com

Nobilis, Inc.
57-A Industrial Rd.
Berkeley Heights, NJ 07922
Telephone 800.464.6670
nobilis.fr

Old Timber Table Company
908 Dragon St.
Dallas, TX 75207
Telephone 214.761.1882
oldtimbertable.com

Old World Weavers
D&D Building
979 Third Ave., 10th Fl.
New York, NY 10022
Telephone 212.355.7186
old-world-weavers.com

Osborne & Little
90 Commerce Rd.
Stamford, CT 06902
Telephone 203.359.1500
osborneandlittle.com

Palecek
The New York Design Center
200 Lexington Ave., Ste. 511
New York, NY 10016
Telephone 212.287.0063
palecek.com

Patina, Inc.
351 Peachtree Hills Ave., N.E.
Atlanta, GA 30304
Telephone 800.635.4365
patinainc.com

Perennials Outdoor Fabrics
140 Regal Row
Dallas, TX 75247
Telephone 214.638.4162
perennialsfabrics.com

Peter Fasano, Ltd.
964 S. Main St.
Great Barrington, MA 01230
Telephone 413.528.6872

Pierre Frey, Ltd.
12 E. 32nd St.
New York, NY 10016
Telephone 212.213.3099

Pindler & Pindler, Inc.
11910 Poindexter Ave.
Moorpark, CA 93021
Telephone 805.531.9090
pindler.com

Pizitz Home & Cottage
121 Central Square
Seaside, FL 32459
Telephone 850.231.2240

Pollack & Associates
150 Varick St.
New York, NY 10013
Telephone 212.627.7766
pollackassociates.com

Prima Seta Silks/Jagtar & Co
3073 N. California St.
Burbank, CA 91505
Telephone 818.729.9333

Quadrille Wallpapers & Fabrics, Inc.
50 Dey Street, Building One
Jersey City, NJ 07306
Telephone 201.792.5959

Randolph & Hein, Inc.
2222 Palou Ave.
San Francisco, CA 94124
Telephone 800.844.9922
raldolphhein.com

Raoul Textiles
8687 Melrose Ave., Ste. G-160
West Hollywood, CA 90069
Telephone 310.657.4931

Reynière Workshop
142 Oak Rd.
Monroe, NY 10950
Telephone 845.774.1541

Robert Allen Fabrics
55 Cabot Blvd.
Mansfield, MA 02048
Telephone 800.240.8189
robertallendesign.com

Roger Arlington, Inc.
30-10 41st Ave., Ste. 2R
Long Island City, NY 11101
Telephone 718.729.5554

Rogers & Goffigon, Ltd.
41 Chestnut St., Ste. 3
Greenwich, CT 06830
Telephone 203.532.8068

Rose Cumming Fabrics
Fine Arts Building
232 E. 59th St., 5th Fl.
New York, NY 10022
Telephone 212.758.0844
rosecumming.com

Rose Tarlow Textiles
8454 Melrose Pl.
Los Angeles, CA 90069
Telephone 323.653.2122
rosetarlow.com

Sea Cloth
107 Greenwich Ave.
Greenwich, CT 06830
Telephone 203.422.6150
seacloth.com

Scalamandré
300 Trade Zone Dr.
Ronkonkoma, NY 11779
Telephone 800.932.4361
scalamandre.com

F. Schumacher Company
79 Madison Ave., 14th Fl.
New York, NY 10016
Telephone 212.213.7900
fschumacher.com

Scully & Scully
504 Park Ave.
New York, NY 1002
Telephone 212.755.2590
scullyandscully.com

Shannon & Jeal
722 Steiner St.
San Francisco, CA 94117
Telephone 415.563.2727
s-j.com

The Silk Trading Co.
360 S. La Brea Ave.
Los Angeles, CA 90036
Telephone 323.954.9280
silktrading.com

Smith & Watson
200 Lexington Ave., Ste. 801
New York, NY 10016
Telephone 212.686.6444
smith-watson.com

Stroheim & Romann, Inc.
30-30 47th Ave.
New York, NY 11101
Telephone 718.706.7000
stroheim.com

Summer Hill, Ltd
2682 Middlefield Rd.
Redwood City, CA 94063
Telephone 650.363.2600
summerhill.com

Travers & Company
504 E. 74th St.
New York, NY 10021
Telephone 212.772.2778
traversinc.com

Zimmer + Rohde
15 Commerce Rd.
Stamford, CT 06902
Telephone 203.327.1400
zimmer-rohde.com

Garden Ornaments

Archiped Classis
315 Cole St.
Dallas, TX 75207
Telephone 214.748.7437
archipedclassics.com

Barbara Israel Garden Antiques
296 Mount Holly Rd.
Katonah, NY 10536
Telephone 212.744.6281
By Appointment Only
bi-gardenantiques.com

Elizabeth Street Garden & Gallery
1172 Second Ave.
New York, NY 10021
Telephone 212.644.6969

Lexington Gardens
1011 Lexington Ave.
New York, NY 10021
Telephone 212.861.4390

Tancredi & Morgan
7174 Carmel Valley Rd.
Carmel Valley, CA 93923
831.625.4477

Treillage, Ltd.
418 E. 75th St.
New York, NY 10021
Telephone 212.535.2288
treillageonline.com

Iron Work

Brun Metal Crafts, Inc.
2791 Industrial Ln.
Bloomfield, CO 80020
Telephone 303.466.2513

Cole Smith, FAIA and ASID
Smith, Ekblad & Associates
2719 Laclede St.
Dallas, TX 75204
Telephone 214.871.0305

Gone are the days of heavy, over-the-top curtains. Instead, Roman shades frame a stairwell while controlling the amount of light invited in.

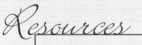

Ironies
2222 Fifth St.
Berkeley, CA 94710
Telephone 510.644.2100
ironies.com

Murray's Iron Work
1801 E. 50th St.
Los Angeles, CA 90058
Telephone 323.521.1100
murraysiw.com

Potter Art Metal
4500 N. Central Expwy.
Dallas, TX 75206
Telephone 214.821.1419
potterartmetal.com

Linens

E. Braun & Co.
717 Madison Ave.
New York, NY 10021
Telephone 212.838.0650
ebraunandco.com

Casa Del Bianco
866 Lexington Ave.
New York, NY 10021
Telephone 212.249.9224

Frette
799 Madison Ave.
New York, NY 10021
Telephone 212.988.5221
frette.com

Léron Linens
804 Madison Ave.
New York, NY 10021
Telephone 800.954.6369
leron.com

Linen Gallery
7001 Preston Rd., Ste. 100
Dallas, TX 75205
Telephone 214.522.6700
linengallery.com

Peacock Alley
4311 Oak Lawn Ave., Ste. 150
Dallas, TX 75219
Telephone 214.520.6736
peacockalley.com

D. Porthault, Inc.
18 E. 69th St.
New York, NY 10021
Telephone 212.688.1660
d-porthault.com

Pratesi
829 Madison Ave.
New York, NY 10021
Telephone 212.288.2315
pratesi.com

Sharyn Blond Linens
2708 W. 53rd St.
Fairway, KS 66208
Telephone 913.362.4420
sharynblondlinens.com

Yves Delorme
1725 Broadway Ave.
Charlottesville, VA 22902
Telephone 800.322.3911
yvesdelorme.com

Lighting, Lamps, and Custom Lamp Shades

Ann Morris Antiques
239 E. 60th St.
New York, NY 10022
Telephone 212.755.3308

Bella Shades/Bella Copia
255 Kansas St.
San Francisco, CA 94103
Telephone 415.255.0452

Brown
2940 Ferndale St.
Houston, TX 77098
Telephone 713.522.2151
theshopbybrown.com

Cele Johnson Custom Lamps
1410 Dragon St.
Dallas, TX 75207
Telephone 214.651.1645

Chandelier
7466 A Girard Ave.
La Jolla, CA 92037
Telephone 858.454.9450

Paul Ferrante, Inc.
8464 Melrose Pl.
Los Angeles, CA 90069
Telephone 323.653.4142
paulferrante.com

Marvin Alexander, Inc.
315 E. 62nd St., 2nd Fl.
New York, NY 10021
Telephone 212.838.2320

Murray's Iron Work
1801 E. 50th St.
Los Angeles, CA 90058
Telephone 323.521.1100
murraysiw.com

Nesle Inc.
38-15 30th St.
Long Island City, NY 11101
Telephone 212.755.0515
nesleinc.com

Niermann Weeks
Fine Arts Building
232 E. 59th St., 1st Fl.
New York, NY 10022
Telephone 212.319.7979
niermannweeks.com

Panache
719 N. La Cienega Blvd.
Los Angeles, CA 90069
Telephone 310.652.5050

Thomas Grant Chandeliers, Inc.
1804 Hi Line Dr.
Dallas, TX 75207
Telephone 214.651.1937

Vaughan Designs, Inc.
979 Third Ave., Ste. 1511
New York, NY 10022
Telephone 212.319.7070
vaughandesigns.com

Stone and Tile

Ann Sacks Tile & Stone Inc.
8120 N.E. 33rd Dr.
Portland, OR 97211
Telephone 800.278.8453
annsacks.com

Architectural Design Resources
2808 Richmond Ave., Ste. E
Houston, TX 77098
Telephone 713.877.8366
adrhouston.com

Country Floors
15 E. 16th St.
New York, NY 10003
Telephone 212.627.8300
countryfloors.com

M.A. Tile & Stone Design
2120 Las Palmas Dr., Ste. H
Carlsbad, CA 92011
Telephone 760.268.0811

Paris Ceramics
151 Greenwich Ave.
Greenwich, CT 06830
Telephone 888.845.3487
parisceramics.com

Renaissance Tile & Bath
349 Peachtree Hills Ave., N.E.
Atlanta, GA 30305
Telephone 800.275.1822
renaissancetileandbath.com

Roof Tile & Slate Company
1209 Carroll St.
Carrollton, Texas 75006
Telephone 972.242.7785
claytile.com

Tesserae Mosaic Studio, Inc.
1111 N. Jupiter Rd., Ste. 108A
Plano, TX 75074
Telephone 972-578-9006
tesseraemosaicstudio.com

Unique Stone Imports
1130 W. Morena Blvd.
San Diego, CA 92110
Telephone 619.275.8300
uniquestoneimports-sd.com

Walker Zanger, Inc.
8901 Bradley Ave.
Sun Valley, CA 91352
Telephone 877.611.0199
walkerzanger.com

Trimmings and Passementerie

Ellen S. Holt, Inc.
1013 Slocum St.
Dallas, TX 75207
Telephone 214.741.1804
ellensholt.com

Houlès USA Inc.
8584 Melrose Ave.
Los Angeles, CA 90069
Telephone 310.652.6171
houles.com

Kenneth Meyer Company
325 Vermont St.
San Francisco, CA 94103
Telephone 415.861.0118

Le Potager
108 W. Brookdale Pl.
Fullerton, CA 92832
Telephone 714.680.8864

Leslie Hannon Custom Trimmings
665 Vetter Ln.
Arroyo Grande, CA 93420
Telephone 805.489.8400
lesliehannontrims.com

Renaissance Ribbons
PO Box 699
Oregon House, CA 95961
Telephone 530.692.0842
renaissanceribbons.com

Samuel & Sons
983 Third Ave.
New York, NY 10022
Telephone 212.704.8000
samuelandsons.com

Tassels & Trims
232 E. 59th St.
New York, NY 10022
Telephone 212.754.6000

West Coast Trimming Corp.
7100 Wilson Ave.
Los Angeles, CA 90001
Telephone 323.587.0701

Thanks to creative hands, a powder room merits a second look. Dallas decorative artist Mike Furmon began by topping humble burlap with plaster and then rolling the fabric, thus causing the plaster to crack. Finally, a tea stain glaze helped yield the impressive results.